Career Planning

Skills to Build Your Future

Clarke G. Carney
The Ohio State University

Cinda Field Wells

Don Streufert

D. VAN NOSTRAND COMPANY

New York   Cincinnati   Toronto   London   Melbourne

Chapter opening quotes

Chapter 1.   Courtesy of J. Bronowski, *The Ascent of Man*, Little, Brown and Company, 1973.

Chapter 2.   Courtesy of Piet Hein, "A Psychological Tip," in *Grooks*, Doubleday and Company, originally the M.I.T. Press, 1966. © by Piet Hein.

Chapter 3.   Boardman.

Chapter 4.   From Ric Masten, "Coming and Going," in *Speaking Poems*, Palo Colorado Press, 1979.

Chapter 5.   Courtesy of Lewis Carroll, *Alice in Wonderland*, Crown Publishers.

Chapter 6.   Courtesy of Piet Hein, "Living is," in *Grooks*, Doubleday and Company, originally the M.I.T. Press, 1966. © by Piet Hein.

Chapter 7.   Jacob A. Riis.

Chapter 8.   Henry Sedgwick.

Preface

How many times have you heard yourself or others say, "But that's not the way I thought things would be. Why didn't someone tell me?" Even after we are "old enough to know better," we expect things to turn out the way movies and fairy tales tell us that they should. The frog turns into a prince; the hero rides off into the sunset. We constantly make choices and go on about our daily business, secure in the fact that we will live happily ever after.

Career choice, a major determining factor in shaping our lives, is one of the decisions most subject to this myth. Most of us grow up believing that we will select an occupation and remain unchanged in our choice as long as we work. Many of us have parents who did exactly that. But, things do change. Along with rapidly growing technology has come the periodic creation and disappearance of whole industries and groups of jobs. Along with increasing affluence has come greater mobility and higher expectations. More and more people are looking for jobs that provide meaning as well as money. Growth and change, then, must be built into any career decision; they are the heartbeat of the process of career planning. We are both producers and products of change. As our goals, interests, and needs change—we try to arrange our work or educational settings to accommodate new visions. We are constantly adapting to changing educational, environmental, and work demands. Sometimes we feel sad about what we must leave behind, but most of the time we are also looking forward to new opportunities.

A number of social scientists have observed that the people who thrive in the midst of change are those who anticipate change, have the skills to deal with it, and, ideally, to take advantage of it. *Career Planning: Skills to Build Your Future* has been written to help you acquire the skills and attitudes to plan effectively for and manage the changes you will experience during your career. We believe that students who are effective in organizing and carrying out their career goals possess five important skills: (1) they are aware of and know how to use several decision-making strategies; (2) they have a clear understanding of their personal interests, values, capabilities, and how those qualities develop and change over time; (3) they understand how the world of work is organized and see the information they gather about different occupations in the light of their own life-style needs and preferences; (4) they can use several strategies for locating and securing employment; (5) they understand the social demands of the workplace. This text presents these skills in an easy to follow sequence in which one skill builds upon another and theory is applied through practical activities.

Career Planning: Skills to Build Your Future starts with a broad view of the historical development of work and examines how your beliefs affect your career decisions. The book then moves to a discussion and an application of skills for proactive decision making. Next, the focus shifts to a broad view of the lifelong process of career development and an identification of the personal qualities that are applicable to the world of work. Self-assessment inventories are used to help you clarify your interests, abilities, and values. From self-awareness, the focus is turned to an overview of the structure and functions of occupations within the world of work today. Effective techniques for gathering information about occupations are presented, and techniques are provided for assessing this information in light of your individual needs and life-style preferences. Personal and occupational exploration come together as the next step in the career planning process through a review of ways of carrying out your career goals through effective strategies for locating and securing employment. These more specific steps are followed by a broad view of the hidden social requirements of the work place and a discussion of how you can continue your self-development through work. Thus, the text completes a circle that starts with self-awareness and ends with self-enrichment. And, that really is our hope: to provide you with an increased sense of self-awareness and practical skills for building your future in a changing world.

Although these materials bear our names, they are the product of the energies of many people. Whenever possible, we have identified and acknowledged the creators and publishers of materials used in this book, and we appreciate their willingness to allow us to adopt their materials to our framework. Two individuals deserve special mention for their contributions to early versions of the text. Russ Sewell deserves recognition for contributing the first draft of "Finding a Job" and for his willingness to accept our revisions. Similar thanks are due Casey Green for "Work Adjustment and Career Expansion."

We would also like to acknowledge the support of our effort by a number of colleagues at The Ohio State University. Professor Joe Quaranta has been a major contributor to our success through the administrative support and encouragement he has given us since the start of our creative journey some five years ago. Carolyn Carder, Bob Kazin, Jackie Vice, Alice J. Tenney, Dianne Greenler, Janice Sutera Wolfe, Karen Taylor, Connie Michele Ward, Lesley Jones,

Louise Douce, and Barbara Benton also contributed greatly through their suggestions for strengthening the materials and our leader-training program.

We would like to thank the following reviewers for reading the manuscript and making helpful comments and suggestions: Reed Mencke, University of Arizona; Robin Raybuck, Cleveland State University; Sharee Schrader, University of Nevada; Louise Douce, The Ohio State University; Jane S. Schachter, Northeastern University; Karen E. McGuire, Northeastern University; and Roger B. Wadsworth, Miami Dade Community College.

Our highest praise is given to those who in typing the manuscript over the years had to put up with our indecisiveness, last minute brainstorms, and often illegible handwriting. Betty Melragen, Betty Reed, Phyllis Demuth, Jean Brethauer, and Carma Kovalo made the effort a bit easier because of their contribution to earlier versions of the text. Lillian Rice and Maryann Marsh helped us complete the task by doing an outstanding job of typing the final draft, often under considerable time pressure. Harriet Serenkin of D. Van Nostrand Company shaped it into its final form through her fine editing.

Lastly, Vicki, Leland, and Mary should receive a warm thanks for their encouragement and for recognizing when to step back as we struggled to fit the pieces together.

Clarke G. Carney
Cinda Field Wells
Don Streufert

Contents

chapter

1

Changing World; Changing Me

Every animal leaves traces of what it was;
man alone leaves traces of what he created.

Jacob Bronowski

This text has been written to help you better understand yourself and our society, so that you can make educational and occupational choices that provide you with a sense of fulfillment and opportunity. To help you see the choices that lie before you more clearly, we believe it will be helpful to understand how our society differs from others. In this way, we hope to give you a sense of how our society's beliefs and ideals work together with our technology. By understanding the origins of our social beliefs and their consequences, each of us can more freely say, "This is what I want. This is what I believe." In that way, we can each make our own choices about how we believe and work.

If we arrange human cultures according to their origins and work activities, we find that they fall along a historical continuum that starts with hunting and gathering societies—probably the first form of human society—passes through agricultural societies, and ends with modern industrial societies. Because each of these societies exists in some form today, the past still lives with us in the present.

HUNTING AND GATHERING SOCIETIES

Hunting and gathering activities extend back at least 20,000 years, probably to our earliest origins, and still exist today in some parts of the world. The natural environment is the primary influence on social and work organization in these societies. Group membership and tribal roles change regularly to adapt to changing needs and environments. Tribes may split or combine membership, depending on available resources. In a few tribes, leadership and hunting roles are assumed by females while males take on family care tasks. Unlike our society, which places high value on individuality and independence, hunting and gathering groups believe that an individual's worth is determined by what he or she contributes to the tribe. One conforms to the natural order of things; one does not attempt to alter them.

Technology plays a very minor role in these societies. Tools are crude, although their creation and ownership is a source of pride. Most dwellings are natural or very simply constructed. Human muscle is the primary source of transportation and power; social organization and cooperation are required to achieve most goals. Some anthropologists believe that societies like these have not changed over time because they must spend their time gathering food. The status quo, however, may also be maintained in part by strong belief in traditions, and by putting group welfare above individual achievement or innovation. This illustrates that, even in these early communities, social beliefs and technology compliment each other.

AGRICULTURAL SOCIETIES

A second style of living emerged some 10,000 years ago in the Middle East and Asia, and about 5,000 years ago among the Incas in Peru. Agricultural and pastoral societies began with the domestication of sheep and goats and the cultivation of crops. This made it possible for tribes to settle in one place, grow larger, and establish villages. The unpredictable environment came under greater control as technology expanded. Land and livestock were harnessed and made to serve more people more conveniently. From this shift in the balance between environment and technology, new divisions of labor and new social values evolved.

The distinction between physical and nonphysical work roles, which still exists today, sprang up in these early communities. Manual labor included tending crops and animals, as well as the handcrafting of household items such as fabric and pottery. Nonphysical roles, which carried greater prestige, revolved around an increased need for protection from the violence of nature and other people and communities. Astronomers predicted weather conditions, priests prayed over them. Carpenters and craftsmen made more durable shelters and implements. Community and judicial officials arbitrated disputes and encouraged community harmony.

Social values in Western European agricultural communities swung gradually away from a focus on group survival, toward an emphasis on closeness and prosperity for each family unit. Living by nature's dictates gave way to a greater ability and desire to intervene in nature for human ends. The equation of prosperity with hard work and integrity became central to the agrarian society's religious and social traditions; so the **"Protestant work ethic"** was born. This life-style, based on hard work, family loyalty, and intervention in nature, is still a cultural basis for many nations of the world, including many areas of the United States.

INDUSTRIAL SOCIETIES

Occurring only 200 years ago with the harnessing of water power and automation, the **Industrial Revolution** created great numbers of new and attractive jobs in urban centers, requiring individual initiative but, at the same time, disconnnecting workers from their families and the land. The unprecedented rate of technological and scientific change following these early successes brought numerous unforeseen options and often confusing consequences. In industrial societies, technology became the primary influence over peoples' lives. Time came to be measured by the clock; it was no longer gauged by natural changes in seasons or social events. Extended families began to split apart as a new emphasis was placed on mobility and personal gain. Old values were soon called into question. As technology continued to conquer environmental limitations, it also challenged and altered the existing social and work organization in complex and far-reaching ways. Prior to the Industrial Revolution, trade skills were passed from generation to generation within families, leading to the development of family surnames such as Miller and Carpenter. When the work setting moved from the home to factory, it became possible for greater numbers of people to enter previously closed occupations. Thus, while members of agricultural and pastoral societies could expect an occupational role to last a lifetime, members of the American industrial society are aware that <u>change is not only possible, it is often unavoidable</u>.

- Forty to 50 percent of the entering university freshman class will not complete college with their classmates. Out of those who remain, 30 to 50 percent will have changed their majors at least once; 15 to 20 percent will have changed their majors two or more times by graduation.

- In the United States, the average 20-year-old man can be expected to change jobs six or seven times during his working life.[1]

- Data from the Decimal Census revealed that almost a third of all workers in 1965 transferred to a different occupation in 1970.

- In the USA, 25 percent of present day workers are in occupations that did not exist 25 years ago. It is estimated that by 1990, 75 percent of the American population will be in jobs that do not yet exist.[1]

- At the beginning of this century, only 3 percent of Americans were over 65 years of age; that figure is now more than 10 percent. The median age of Americans during the last decade increased from 26.0 to 29.4 and, according to the Federal Bureau of Census, it will reach 32.5 by the year 2000.

- The number of mothers in the USA who hold paid jobs has more than doubled in the past two decades. If the present trend continues, by 1980 the majority of mothers will hold outside jobs in addition to their family responsibilities.

- At the rate knowledge is accumulating, by the time the child born today completes his or her education, the amount of knowl-

1. From B. Hopson and P. Hough, *Exercises in Personal and Career Development*, New York: APS Publications, 1973, p. 22.

edge in the world will be four times greater than now. By the time that individual is 50, it will be 32 times greater, and 97 percent of the knowledge in the world will have been acquired within his lifetime.[1]

Because change is constant in American society, lifelong learning through continuing education has become a necessity, bringing people of diverse ages and backgrounds back to the classroom. Some individuals are new to the work force (largely women), some are changing jobs, and some are upwardly mobile within their fields. Others are required to accumulate continued education in order to keep their present jobs. All of these phenomena cause the educational level of our population to spiral upward.

Old standards for what work is appropriate for men and women are also being questioned in our society. An ever increasing number of women are participating in the labor force, and many are staying single and seeking the same rewards and status positions traditionally accorded to men. The American Council on Life Insurance reports that the proportion of women between the ages of 25 and 29 who remain unmarried has increased by more than a third since 1960.

As increasing numbers of women and members of minority groups seek their place in the labor force, they run into old beliefs about who should benefit from the gains of industrialization. While the Industrial Revolution served to democratize the world of work for a great number of males, it did not do so for women. Prior to the Industrial Revolution a form of coequality existed between male and female family members. Each sex contributed to the goods and services the family exchanged with other community members to meet their needs. When the Industrial Revolution occurred, males began to work outside of the home for pay, and consequently took on the familiar breadwinner roles. Being privy to more information about what was happening in the society, the male had more direct influence over social issues. The female, on the other hand, was assigned the task of managing the home and could influence the socio-economic issues of the day only by influencing the opinions of her male relatives. Because of economic class membership, racism, and other social barriers, certain racial and ethnic minority groups were also excluded from full participation in the society.

These historical events continue to trouble us today. Although our social insititutions have—with some success—attempted to break down old barriers that prohibited the full economic participation of women and minorities, old cultural attitudes and beliefs serve as a source of continued social tension during this time of change.

Until recently, participation in the American economy was restricted for women and minorities, who had access to only a limited number of occupations. Because of old beliefs about the role of women and minorities in our society, a disproportionate number of women and black males still work in low-paying occupations, especially those that provide service to others such as teaching, nursing, and social services.

Due to their long-standing isolation from our society's professional and managerial ranks, it is not hard to understand why many women and minority group members are frustrated and flounder, even though affirmative action laws have opened new doors for them. Their occupational tradition has been one of serving others; now we are asking them to be comfortable and to compete in situations that require individual achievement, managing others, and control of their environments. Such a complete shift cannot be made overnight. Old beliefs about one's roles and those of others change gradually, and new skills to meet the requirements of new opportunities take time to develop. Perhaps the most significant thing each of us can do is to be patient and support each other's efforts at constructive change.

SKILLS FOR MANAGING CHANGE

In looking at these three different kinds of societies, it becomes clear how work has many different meanings to different people. For the hunter and gatherer there are few choices about what one can do with his or her life, and choices are usually dictated by a person's gender. Those living in agricultural and pastoral societies have more choices, largely centered on the limited range of possibilities in the community and on family traditions.

Those of us who live in the industrial societies have the greatest range of choices. But, unlike our counterparts in other ways of life, we also have greater personal responsibility for our choices. While many of us go by the dictates of our families in selecting an academic major or an occupation, the tug to be your own person and make an independent choice still exists. We have also seen that, unlike youth in other societies where choices tend to be more permanent, American youth are likely to face the need to reexamine their occupational directions several times throughout their working lives.

How can we plan for the future now, yet remain open to change as our needs and goals—and those of our society—evolve over time? This is a question that must be answered for effective career planning to occur. We believe the answer is to develop the skills now that prepare you for a lifetime of career decision making. By doing this, you will be able to anticipate and effectively manage your growth in a changing world.

Regardless of whether you are making a choice for now, or new choices in the future, you will need to master five essential career planning skills. This text is organized around each of these five skill areas. *The first skill you will need to understand and develop is that of effective decision making.* Our decisions form a bridge between our wants and needs and the world around us. We shape our lives through our decisions. Every day each of us makes a great many decisions; some require little thought and planning, others require a great deal. Whether your decisions are large or small, if you have not developed the skills for effective decision making you may find yourself feeling powerless and directionless. Chapter Two, "Making Career Decisions: Self-Stages and Strategies," will help you focus on and refine your career decision making skills.

The process of effective career decision making begins and ends with ourselves; with the way we shape our worlds to accommodate our unique capabilities, interests, and values. *The second essential skill for career planning thus involves the ability to pull together the many pieces of information you have about yourself to create a picture of who you are occupationally.* Since you are likely to change as you mature and gain work experience, the images you have of yourself are more like the frames in a motion picture than a snapshot. You will need to plan for an ongoing self-review process, including feedback about your skills and interests from others and observations provided through self-assessment inventories. By providing you with the ability to organize information about yourself, and the understanding of how your goals, dreams, and needs are likely to change over the course of your career, we hope to better prepare you for managing your own career development. Chapter Three, "The Emerging Self: Birth to Adolescence," and Chapter Four, "The Emerging Self: Beyond Adolescence," provide an in depth exploration of how personal and environmental influences shape the course of a person's career.

The third essential skill is that of gathering and assessing occupational information. Most of us are familiar with a number of occupations, but probably only a few of us have a real sense of how seemingly unrelated occupations fit together forming unified industries and economic networks. Like one piece of a puzzle, each occupation shares characteristics in common with the pieces around it. As you acquire knowledge of the whole puzzle, you will begin to better understand how your particular talents and interests may be used in a variety of settings. By teaching you skills for gathering accurate occupational information, we hope to be able to help you identify

several areas or occupations that suit your work and life-style preferences. Two chapters are devoted to gathering and exploring occupational information. Chapter Five, "Paths in the Workplace,"
provides an overview of the structure of the world of work. Chapter
Six, "It All Has To Do With Needs and Styles," explores how occupational information can be used to assess the life-styles associated
with different jobs and professions.

Having polished your decision making skills, and clarified how
your interests and talents may be used in a number of occupational
settings, you will probably find yourself moving toward making a
commitment to a specific educational or occupational goal. While we
do not believe that all students should or must make a career choice
after reading these materials, we do encourage you to learn and
practice the skills of implementing a career objective through a job
campaign. Doing so will allow you to implement a career objective
effectively when you are ready. *Thus, the fourth essential career planning
skill is one of marketing your skills to employers.* To do so effectively you
will need to learn how to identify potential sources of employment
and market yourself to employers through correspondence, prepared
resumes, and person-to-person interviews. Finding a job requires
hard work. Chapter Seven, "Finding a Job is a Job," will provide
some skills to make the effort easier.

Our society exerts a tremendous pressure on us to be able to adapt
flexibly and effectively to a variety of interpersonal situations. At
different times during our working lives we will be called on to fill
the roles of student, trainee, colleague, instructor, and supervisor.
Each of these roles requires that we be sensitive to our needs and
those of others; to recognize differences and commonalities with
others; to be dependent, independent, and interdependent as the
need arises. Difficulties in mastering these requirements in work are
reflected in the often cited statistic that the primary reason people
lose or fail to get jobs is not technical incompetence but the inability
to get along or work harmoniously with other people. *Recognizing
this, the fifth and final career planning skill that we will be exploring is that
of work adjustment.* Chapter Eight, "Work Adjustment and Career
Expansion," is devoted to this topic. Skills that will be highlighted
in that chapter include managing the interpersonal demands of the
job setting, and promoting your career development by taking advantage of new learning opportunities.

These five skills—decision making, self-assessment, occupational
exploration, job campaigning, and work adjustment and career expansion—form the core of this text. We believe that they are essential
to a self-directed life. We emphasize that they are skills that can be

learned, just like learning to follow a recipe or repair a car. We will develop them through instruction and practice; you can use them over and over again in similar or new situations. When we purchase a car, for example, we practice the skills of deciding for ourselves based on our wants and needs, gathering accurate and reliable information about the car, and locating and securing financial support through applications to creditors. After the car is purchased, we call upon the skills of others and develop our own skills to adjust and maintain the car at its maximal level of efficiency. Finally, just as we look to advance in our career, when the car no longer suits our needs, we recycle through the decision making process and develop new options for ourselves. The person who masters these skills can look forward to a world of change with hope and optimism, and with confidence in his or her resources.

Let us start then at the beginning of the career planning cycle, with an understanding of the process of decision making. The activity that follows will help you to explore how the beliefs you currently hold about yourself and the world of work may affect the way you go about making career decisions. You will also learn a method of challenging and changing beliefs that may restrict your effectiveness and dampen your enthusiasm for making career decisions.

REMOVING *ATTITUDINAL* BLOCKS TO *CAREER* DECISION *MAKING*[2]

Conventional wisdom tells us that we get what we expect from our lives. It is easy to find many examples of this in our everyday decisions and actions. If we are preoccupied with failure, we may make hasty and uninformed decisions and create disasters for ourselves. These may include freezing on an exam, making plans to be at two places at once, or ruining a social activity by putting our wost foot forward.

Many of these stressful events are caused by beliefs or ideas we hold that may lead us to exaggerate a situation, misinterpret circumstances, or otherwise cause us not to get the best outcomes from our efforts. The psychologist Albert Ellis calls such beliefs "irrational" because they hinder us in taking an objective and realistic view of a situation. He suggests that irrational beliefs are often tied to the

---

2. This activity was previously published by Clarke Carney in *Counseling and Human Development.* Vol. 11, No. 4, December, 1978, Denver, Colorado: Love Publishing Company. (Reprinted by permission.)

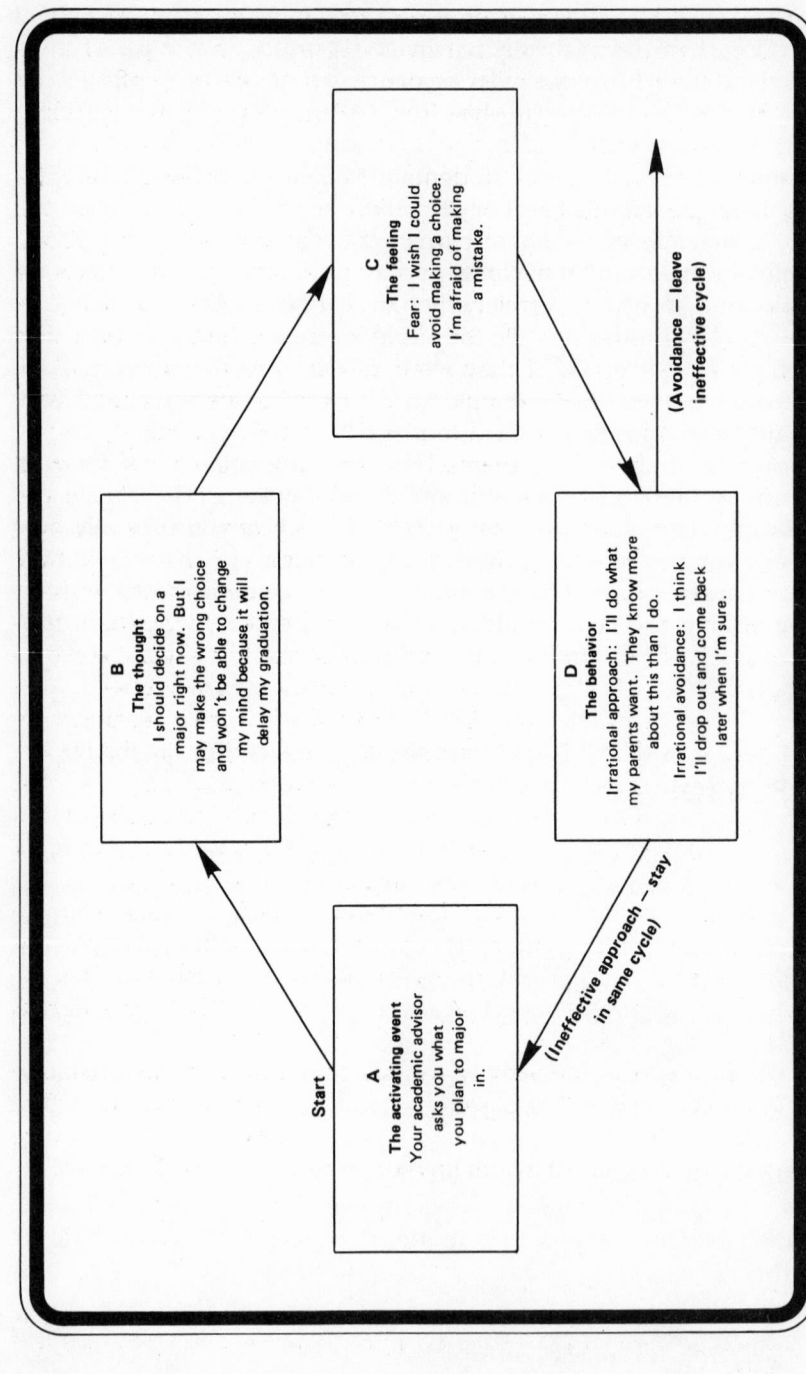

C
The feeling
Fear: I wish I could avoid making a choice. I'm afraid of making a mistake.

B
The thought
I should decide on a major right now. But I may make the wrong choice and won't be able to change my mind because it will delay my graduation.

D
The behavior
Irrational approach: I'll do what my parents want. They know more about this than I do.
Irrational avoidance: I think I'll drop out and come back later when I'm sure.

(Avoidance — leave ineffective cycle)

(Ineffective approach — stay in same cycle)

A
The activating event
Your academic advisor asks you what you plan to major in.

Start

Figure 1.1 Example of an Irrational ABCD decision-making episode.

notions we have about success and failure; what we think we should or shouldn't be doing with our lives. When we follow such beliefs rigidly without checking their accuracy, we can become inflexible in our thinking and block ourselves from finding creative ways of dealing with new situations.

Much of the discomfort students experience in making career decisions is caused by beliefs or ideas they have about career planning that are not accurate or not current. As we have seen, our beliefs about what we should be doing in our careers are shaped by the ever changing nature of our society. Sometimes our society can change so rapidly that it takes a while for our individual beliefs and standards to catch up, especially if they were taught to us by members of an older generation. For example, our society offers students many options and encourages them to make their own individual choices. Thus, while students see themselves as having a number of personal career options, many are still influenced by the old belief that the choice of a vocation will last a lifetime. As a result, they may feel anxious about making a career decision because they believe they must find the one right and permanent occupation for themselves. The activity that follows identifies this and other inaccurate or irrational beliefs that can operate in career decisions, making the choice of an educational or vocational objective a distressing problem.

This activity teaches the ABCD method of problem analysis developed by Donald Tosi[3] to assist people who want to change behaviors they are uncomfortable with. It is based on the premise that when an environmental event occurs, you filter it through a series of ideas and beliefs which in turn generate a series of positive or negative feelings. These feelings cause you to make a choice and act in ways that either move you toward or away from an appropriate or effective response. The cycle completes itself when your behavior confirms your original interpretation of the situation and you do indeed get what you expect. An example of the ABCD paradigm is shown in Figure 1.1.

The first part of the activity will teach you how to identify faulty or irrational beliefs that currently affect your career planning. The second part will teach you how to correct those beliefs and change your decisions and behaviors toward more rewarding directions.

3. Donald J. Tosi. Self-directed behavior change in the cognitive, affective, and behavioral motoric domains: A Rational-Emotive Approach. *Focus On Guidance*, December, 1973.

PART ONE: THE ABCD IRRATIONAL CAREER PLANNING SEQUENCE

These first four steps are designed to help you analyze more precisely personal sources of discomfort or conflict that affect your career planning.

A **Step One: Possible Activating Events**

The process of career decision making and career planning involves a series of steps from early exploration, to commitment, and finally to action. Each one of these steps may serve as an activating event that invites irrational decision making. Some of these events are listed below. No doubt you will discover others as you work through your career plans. Spaces are provided so you can lengthen or modify this list. Pick three activating events from the list below that apply to you. Rank them from most to least upsetting and write them under A (*Activating Events*) in Figure 1.2.

1. Graduating from high school and being faced with the choice between college and work.
2. Graduating from high school and having to decide between colleges.
3. Being asked to declare a major on the college application form.
4. Seeing the results of a National Admissions Exam and realizing how you compare with other college bound individuals in your major.
5. Being asked to declare a major in order to register for another quarter.
6. Being asked what you plan to do with the rest of your life.
7. Having to plan a class schedule.

C **Step Two: Undesirable Emotional or Affective States**

The following is a partial list of emotional states that people often associate with career decision making. Try to identify the feelings that you experience as accompanying the *Activating Events* (A's) that have influenced your current career decision making. Record these under C (*Undesirable Emotions*) in Figure 1.2.

	Least emotionally upsetting		Most emotionally upsetting
A. Activating events (A's)			Seeing results of GRE and realizing how I compare with other Ph.D. applicants
B. Irrational beliefs, philosophies, thoughts. "What I think" (B's)			If I wait a year before applying, I'll be better prepared. In order to feel worthwhile, I have to be competent...
C. Undesirable emotions. "What I feel" (C's)			anxious inadequate like I've failed
D. Undesirable behaviors "What I do" (D's)			- I procrastinate applying for Ph.D. prgms - I stop trying to get in prgms - I put myself down

Figure 1.2   ABCD problem analysis—Part One: Complete by following steps in Part One.

13

1. I feel angry or irritable.
2. I feel anxious, worried, and fearful.
3. I feel bored or dull.
4. I feel like I've failed.
5. I feel frustrated.
6. I feel guilty or self-condemning.
7. I feel hopeless or depressed.
8. I feel all alone.
9. I feel helpless or inadequate.
10. I feel self-pity.
11. I feel worthless or inferior.
12. I feel resentful.
13. I feel lazy.
14. I feel vulnerable.
15. I feel foolish.
16. I feel rigid or stuck.
17. I feel dependent.
18. I feel cautious.

Step Three: Undesirable Behaviors, Actions, or Habits

The following behaviors tend to be self-defeating and inappropriate for effective career planning, especially if they appear with great intensity or regularity. From this list, select those behaviors that you are likely to engage in as a consequence of the *Activating Events* (A's) you specified and the *Undesirable Emotions* (C's) you have identified in Figure 1.2. Record these under *Undesirable Behaviors* (D's) on Figure 1.2. Describe your behavior as specifically as you can.

1. I avoid responsibility for the choice.
2. I procrastinate or postpone the choice.
3. I withdraw.
4. I do not gather the necessary information for making a decision.
5. I gather information but do not have any criteria for evaluating its relevance to me.
6. I allow others to make the choice for me.
7. I get stomach aches or show other signs of anxiety.
8. I declare a choice without fully exploring it.
9. I make up a class schedule without seeing my advisor.
10. I do not study or prepare.
11. I go on unemployment.
12. I put myself down in front of others.
13. I act guilty.
14. I frequently change my mind.
15. I stay in the undecided curriculum until an advisor pushes for a decision.
16. I explore excessively without deciding.
17. I chose a major or a job that is beyond my abilities.

18. I chose a major or a job that is below my abilities.
19. I frequently drop classes.
20. I become a professional student.
21. I ask a counselor for a test that will tell me what to do with my life.
22. I do not prepare a resume or cover letter.
23. I slap together a resume or cover letter with little thought.
24. I do not use the placement office to locate job possibilities.
25. I avoid employment interviews.
26. I perform poorly during an interview.
27. I stay in a job or family situation even though I am dissatisfied.
28. I set myself up to fail.
29. I do not really try, so I can't really fail.

Step Four: The Irrational Beliefs or Ideas

A great number of irrational beliefs operate to cause undesirable actions in career planning. The following is a partial list of some of the more commonly held irrational beliefs that college students have about the process of career planning. From this list, select those *Irrational Beliefs* (B's) that occur between the *Activating Events* (A's) and the *Undesirable Emotions* (C's) you experience in your own career decision making. List them in the space provided under *Irrational Beliefs* (B's) in Figure 1.2.

1. The choice of a major or occupation is irreversible. Once you make it you cannot change your mind.
2. There is a single right career for everyone.
3. It is not okay to be undecided since being undecided is a sign of immaturity.
4. Nobody else is undecided. I'm all alone.
5. Somewhere there is a test that can tell me what to do with the rest of my life.
6. I know other people who have known what they wanted to be since childhood. Something's wrong with me because I can't be that way.
7. Others know what's best for me.
8. Somewhere there is an expert who can tell me what to do.
9. Everyone must climb the ladder of success even if it means doing things that do not interest you.

10. If you can find out what you are interested in, you'll automatically do well at it.

11. You must thoroughly analyze all aspects of a choice before you implement it, otherwise you're not really prepared.

12. People are either successful or complete failures in their career pursuits. There's no in-between.

13. If I get away from the pressure to decide—if I take a year or two off from college—I'll make a better decision.

14. Go where the money is, regardless of what kind of work it involves.

15. The world of work is changing so rapidly that you really can't plan for the future.

16. We should respect tradition and maintain different types of work for men and women.

17. If things don't go the way I expect, it means that I'm a failure.

18. In order to have a feeling of worth, I should be and must be thoroughly competent, adequate, intelligent, and achieving in all possible respects.

19. Work is the only real way to personal fulfillment.

20. If I say no to what others expect of me, I'll be insensitive and unlovable.

21. I'm unhappy when I think about selecting a career goal because things external to me make me that way.

22. A person should be in total control of his or her career.

23. I must choose between really having a career and having a family.

24. Women shouldn't compete with men for jobs, especially those that involve creativity, managing others, and decision making. Since they are passive, emotional, and respond to things intuitively, women just aren't equipped to handle such situations.

25. If I lose a job to a woman, it means I'm inadequate as a male.

26. If my spouse has to go to work, it means I've failed as a husband.

27. Life is always fair.

28. Life is always unfair.

PART TWO: THE RECONSTRUCTION PROCESS

The central theme of the rational–emotive change theory is that our beliefs dictate our feelings and behaviors. The theory also suggests that by becoming aware of illogical and unrealistic patterns of thought and challenging them, we can replace them with more realistic forms of thinking, more positive feelings, and more constructive behaviors. Based on this idea, this section will (1) attempt to help you correct any irrational ideas you may have about career planning and (2) help you find more satisfying ways of thinking, feeling, and acting as you pursue a career objective.

Purpose of this Section

Step One: Developing More Rational Beliefs

The following section (1) groups the irrational beliefs of the Part One activities according to their common themes, (2) points out evidence that contradicts them, and (3) provides alternative rational beliefs that contradict the irrational beliefs you listed previously in Figure 1.2. Read through the sets of irrational beliefs provided below, the evidence that contradicts them, and the more rational beliefs that the contradictory evidence lead to. Use Section B of Figure 1.3 (*Rational Ideas*), to record the rational beliefs that you wish to substitute for the irrational beliefs you listed in Figure 1.2.

1. *Irrational Belief* The choice of a major or occupation is irreversible. Once you make it you cannot nor should not change your mind.

   The Facts Several surveys of college students have shown that from 30% to 50% of an entering freshman class will change their majors at least once by graduation. Thus, changing one's mind is a pervasive experience in the student population. The belief in irreversible choices stems from the idea that because most academic programs have lock step requirements, a person will lose time and credits if he or she gets out of step with other students in the program. True, one does run the risk of losing time and having to make up credits, and it does cost money to postpone graduating. However, the hidden costs of not leaving a major or occupation one is uncomfortable with are also great in terms of job dissatisfaction, personal stress, and poor performance. Thus, short-term avoidance of inconvenience can lead to long-range heartaches.

   A More Rational Belief Regardless of how carefully I plan an occupation or academic choice, there is always some risk of dissatisfaction because I cannot know all the consequences of a choice. Therefore, I'll need to study the prospects carefully, bearing in mind my own needs and strengths. I'll follow the belief that commitment and action are better than inaction, and prepare to review and perhaps renegotiate my decision at a later time.

	Least emotionally upsetting		Most emotionally upsetting
A. Activating events (A's)			Seeing results of GRE test and realizing how I compared with other students for Ph.D.
B. Rational beliefs, philosophies, thoughts. "What I think" (B's)			
C. Desirable emotions. "What I feel" (C's)			
D. Desirable behaviors "What I do" (D's)			

Figure 1.3   ABCD problem analysis—Part Two: Complete by following steps in Part Two.

2. *Irrational Belief* There is a single right career choice for everyone.

The Facts The belief that there is an ideal occupation in everyone's life originated with the religious notion that one's choice of a vocation demonstrated a calling from God. The U.S. Department of Labor's *Dictionary of Occupational Titles* lists some 20,000 occupations grouped according to skill requirements. A cursory examination of these occupations indicates that certain groups share common skills. Thus, a given individual may have the talents and interests to perform well at a variety of occupations. Although large numbers of persons perform the same work throughout their lives, the odds indicate that most students will try out several occupations or work settings during their careers. Trial lawyers can become teachers, social service administrators, and artists. Some engineers have become physicians and psychologists.

A More Rational Belief The choice of an occupation is but one step in a career that I'll be able to review with certainty only at the end of my working life. Part of the enjoyment of my own growth will be recognizing my need to change as I develop new skills and interests, and to try new things through work including the changing of my original occupational goals.

3. *Irrational Beliefs* It is not okay to be undecided. Being undecided is a sign of immaturity. A variation on this theme: Nobody else is undecided. I'm all alone. A third variation on this theme is: Other people have known what they want to do since childhood. Something's wrong with me because I can't be that way.

The Facts As we noted above, 30% to 50% of the students in a college class will change their majors at least once. Thus, there appear to be a lot of immature students who don't share their undecidedness with each other. In reality, undecidedness is a natural fact of life for most of us irrespective of our age or academic status. All of this suggests the obvious point that the process of living and growing is one of continued exploration, decision, and redecision. Not to decide is nonetheless a decision, and is perhaps the wisest decision a person can make under certain circumstances.

A More Rational Belief Immaturity and undecidedness are not the same thing. It's okay to be undecided, many of my peers are. The important thing is that I make the best use of the resources

I have available so I can make the proper kind of decision when I'm ready to.

4. *Irrational Beliefs*   Somewhere there is a test or an expert who can tell me what to do with the rest of my life. This theme has other variations: Others know what is best for me. If I say no to what others expect of me, I'll be demonstrating that I'm insensitive and unlovable.

The Facts   Again, the *Dictionary of Occupational Titles* lists some 20,000 occupations. Most interest and aptitude inventories sample no more than 200 of these 20,000 occupations. Thus, tests can suggest general areas to explore, but should not be construed as the last word. In fact, statistics show that the best indicator of what a person will do occupationally is what the person says he or she will do, not what tests say. This suggests that even the experts have their limits and are best able to help you find trends in your occupational personal style and to teach you how to gather current and accurate information so you can make up your own mind. You need not be viewed as uncaring if you elect to do something different than others advise, including well-intentioned family and friends who would like to think that they know more than the experts when it comes to planning your future.

A More Rational Belief   What I do with my life will always be my choice. I'll solicit feedback about my interests and talents from others and from tests to get some ideas for exploration, but what I do with that information is really up to me.

5. *Irrational Belief*   If you find out what you are interested in, you'll automatically do well at it.

The Facts   This belief treats one's interests (what you would like to do) and aptitudes (what you can do) as though they were the same. It implies that motivation generated by interests can compensate for deficiencies in one's abilities. While the motivation to do well in a given area can overcome deficiencies, the connection between the two is not one-to-one; being good at something doesn't necessarily imply that you enjoy it, and liking something doesn't mean that you will do well at it.

A More Rational Belief   In my search for an educational or occupational goal I must keep in mind that the most satisfying choice will combine the best aspects of my interests and talents. Using either alone as a criterion for choice can invite frustration later on.

6. *Irrational Beliefs*   A number of irrational beliefs play on a theme of personal control: You must thoroughly analyze all aspects of a choice before you implement it, othewise you're not really prepared. People are either successful or complete failures in their careers. There's no in between. If things don't go the way I expect, it means I'm a failure. In order to have a feeling of worth, I should be and must be thoroughly competent, adequate, intelligent, and achieving in all possible respects. A person should be in total control of his or her career.

The Facts   Even the most advanced sciences admit errors in prediction. Ours is a probablistic world that cannot be totally predicted or controlled. At best we can only guess what the future will be like based on the information we have available now. Success in this sense is relative; it recognizes that errors will be made, and admits to shades of gray. The odds are that we all will have some successes and some failures—it's a matter of degree, not of kind.

A More Rational Belief   Although I cannot fully control the future, I can increase the odds of my best guesses being more accurate. I'm likely to err sometimes but I've got to guess about possible alternatives and their consequences. If I hang myself up on the idea of being perfect, I'll never do anything.

7. *Irrational Beliefs*   The world of work is changing so rapidly that you really can't plan the future. I'm unhappy when I think about selecting a career goal because things external to me make me that way. Life is either always fair or unfair.

The Facts   Unlike the irrational beliefs discussed under 6 above, (which focused on the issue of personal control), these beliefs take the opposite view and focus on external events as controlling forces. Taken in the extreme, both are irrational. While we do not have total control over our futures, we don't lack some control. We take on more control in our lives when we look for continuity in change. Even though some jobs may become obsolete, the structure of the world of work remains basically the same. The best prediction for the immediate future is that which we observe now. Again, we are playing with probability, not certainty. We can increase the odds in our favor by staying on top of labor trends.

A More Rational Belief   Informed action is better than passive inaction or reaction. Keeping abreast of labor trends and changes in myself, I can better prepare for and accommodate changes while still utilizing my natural talents and interests.

8. *Irrational Belief* If I get away from the pressure to decide—if I "stop out" and take a year or two off from college—I'll make a better decision.

    The Facts While taking time away from a problem can sometimes provide added clarity, the mere passage of time will not produce a solution. What time can provide is the opportunity for planful self- and occupational exploration.

    A More Rational Belief My time away from the pressures of a decision can be well spent if I plan for ways of getting the new information I need to make the decision. Before I decide to "stop out," I had better identify exactly what information I need and see if leaving college is the best way of obtaining it.

9. *Irrational Beliefs* Work as the major source of personal fulfillment gets played as a theme in several ways: Everyone must climb the ladder of success, even if it means doing things that do not interest you. Go where the money is, regardless of what you are doing, at least you'll be secure. Work is the only way to personal fulfillment.

    The Facts Work has many connotations to many different people. For some it is indeed the benchmark of personal success. However, for others it supports a personal life-style and thus has secondary importance to their leisure and interpersonal pursuits. The value of work to each individual is a matter of personal choice. Thus, success is a relative notion decided on by each individual, given his or her life goals and life-style preference.

    A More Rational Belief Before I decide on what type of work I want to do and how high I want to climb on the career ladder, I had better decide what kind of life-style I prefer and what it will take to achieve it financially.

10. *Irrational Belief* The woman's place theme has several variations: We should respect tradition and maintain different types of work for men and women. I must choose between really having a career and having a family. Women shouldn't compete with men for jobs, especially those that involve creativity, managing others, and decision making. Since they are passive, emotional, and respond to things intuitively, women aren't equipped to

handle such situations. If I lose a job to a woman, it means I'm inadequate as a male. If my spouse has to go to work, it means I've failed as a husband.

The Facts   While it is true that certain physical limitations can restrict the performance of some women and men at some jobs, many of the beliefs that exist in society about a person's place are based on misinformation and stereotypes. Fortunately, equal rights legislation has done a great deal to level some of these false beliefs by providing opportunities based on merit and skill, not bias. Even given such legislation, it will be important for each individual to carefully check out his or her biases before rejecting any occupation from consideration.

A More Rational Belief   Before I reject any occupation as being unsuitable for me, I had better check out my own biases and those within my environment because of possible inaccuracies in the information I have obtained or inaccuracies in my own beliefs.

Step Three: Positive Emotions

The following list consists of positive or desired emotions that can vary according to their frequency, intensity, and duration. They all share in common the self-enhancing quality of making an individual feel good and reinforcing the positive aspects of decision making. Imagine what it would be like to experience each of the emotions given on the list and try to identify which of them are most likely to be associated with the *Rational Beliefs* (B) that follow the *Activating Events* (A) you recorded in Figure 1.3. Record your choices under C (*Desirable Emotions*) in Figure 1.3

1. Relaxed
2. Joyful
3. Worthwhile
4. Happy
5. Confident
6. Guiltless
7. Hopeful
8. Shameless
9. Elated
10. Energetic
11. Cheerful
12. Dependable
13. Independent
14. Planful
15. Able
16. Patient
17. Trusting
18. Satisfied
19. Stable
20. Knowledgeable
21. Active
22. Competent

Step Four: Desirable Behavior, Actions, or Habits

The behaviors listed below are generally described as desirable, growth-producing, and self-enhancing. Persons who engage in these behaviors tend to see themselves as confident, competent, independent, and on top of their careers. Select those behaviors from the list that you believe are likely to occur as a consequence of using more rational ways of thinking about the activating events of Figure 1.3 and the feelings they produce. Record them under D (*Desirable Behaviors*) on Figure 1.3. Imagine what it would be like for you to engage in these desirable behaviors.

1. Making decisions on my own.
2. Gathering and assessing occupational information by using a self-determined set of criteria.
3. Preparing for an exam with time to spare.
4. Talking through my educational and vocational plans with my advisor or counselor.
5. Volunteering or working part-time in an area related to my career objectives.
6. Taking classes that are consistent with my abilities.
7. Taking classes that will build up skills necessary for my major.
8. Declaring a major.
9. Preparing a one-year plan to continue exploring or building upon a choice.
10. Acting confidently about my goals for future exploration should I elect to "decide not to decide."
11. Talking through my educational and vocational plans with my family.
12. Establishing a long-range plan for exploring career possibilities should I decide to stop out.
13. Planning through and preparing a resume and cover letter with the assistance of a placement office.
14. Attending a job interviewing skills workshop.
15. Preparing an effective job search campaign.

Step Five: New Action Steps

Use the spaces on page 25 to list the thoughts, emotions, and behaviors related to your career planning that you would like to change after completing this exercise.

_____

_____

_____

_____

_____

_____

Now, list the strategies or solutions you plan to use that will help
you in achieving more desirable thoughts, feelings, and actions in
your career planning:

What I can do right now:

1. _____

2. _____

3. _____

4. _____

What I can do by a week from today:

1. _____

2. _____

3. _____

4. _____

What I can do in a month:

1. _____

2. _____

3. _____

4. _____

What I can do when I graduate from or leave college:

1. _____

2. _____

REFERENCES

Bronowski, J. *The Ascent of Man*. Boston: Little, Brown, and Company, 1973.

Downs, James F. *Cultures in Crisis*. Beverly-Hills, California: Glencoe Press, 1971.

Hopson, B. and Hough, P. *Exercises in Personal and Career Development*. New York: APS Publications, 1973.

Neff, W. S. *Work and Human Behavior*. New York: Atherton Press, 1968.

Nobles, W. W. The Negro Self-Concept and Scientific Colonialism. *Black Psychologist*, Summer, 1974.

Making Career Decisions: Self, Strategies, and Stages

A Psychological Tip

Whenever you're called on to make up your mind,
    and you're hampered by not having any,
the best way to solve the dilemma, you'll find,
    is simply by spinning a penny.

No—not so that chance shall decide the affair
    while you're passively standing there moping,
but the moment the penny is up in the air,
    you suddenly know what you're hoping.

Piet Hein

Our self-concepts—the images that come to mind when we ask ourselves, "Who am I?"—provide the strands of continuity we experience as we grow and change. Our self-concepts are most evident in the decisions we make and the actions we take. They reflect the cumulative wisdom gained from our past experiences. Any marked change in our lives challenges our self-concepts and causes feelings of uncertainty. Graduating from college, changing majors, taking a new job, getting married, moving, being promoted, or going on vacation are all common changes that most of us deal with during our lives. Each of these changes requires us to make decisions that reflect our self-concepts.

Even though we may not be aware of it, our decisions are based on our specific beliefs, attitudes, and values, which are woven into the fabric of our self-concepts. These are shaped by messages received and behaviors observed in our family and culture. As we explored in the preceding chapter, our beliefs represent our personal views about how the world operates. Our attitudes, on the other hand, predispose us to like some situations or people and not to like others. Since we cannot have direct experience in every area, many of our attitudes and beliefs are based on information from others even though such information may be distorted or inaccurate. Our values tell us what we should or should not do. What we define as right or proper is a reflection of our values. Our values are also shaped by the society in which we live, by parents, teachers and friends. These influences, then, affect our decisions indirectly through our beliefs, attitudes, and values.

Owing to the changing nature of our society, each of us must frequently try to balance what we now have against what we think will exist in the future; between wanting to keep things secure as they are, and wanting to reshape our lives. In making decisions, each of us must be willing to say, "This is what I value," by freely choosing to give up some options and by assuming the responsibility for the consequences of our choices. We are free to choose and to take responsibility for our choices only when we have two or more options to select from and are capable of acting. Lacking choices and the ability to act, we cannot make real decisions.

In all likelihood, most of our choices will not be permanent. Living involves growth and change; the future holds twists and turns which we cannot predict. While the decisions we make in adjusting to changing life events may be looked at separately, each of our decisions is actually a link in a long chain of choices. Each decision we make builds on our previous decisions and in turn stimulates and influences our future decisions. In looking at an individual decision, it is important to distinguish between the *decision process* and the *decision outcome*. The decision-making process is irreversible in the sense that time cannot be reversed. It propels us forward through a series of decision steps. The outcomes of our decisions—the actions we take and their consequences—often can be changed by making new decisions as new alternatives become available.

The quality of our decisions is affected by the information we use in making them. If we lack the proper information we can run into blind alleys. If we fail to consider carefully all available information we can limit the number of alternatives we consider or make a premature choice. Furthermore, the information we use may be distorted because it is outdated or misrepresented by its source. We, ourselves, can unwittingly distort information because of our personal beliefs, attitudes, and values. Finally, new information may change our decisions. Suppose you were planning to spend your summer working at a camp, for example, only to find out after talking to your academic advisor that you will need to take classes during the summer to graduate on schedule. Instead of facing the single decision of how to obtain a camp job, you would now need to decide between camp and graduation.

LEARNING HOW TO DECIDE

The situations that require us to make decisions will vary greatly throughout our lives. The pressure to change or to decide may come from ourselves, or from the environment—sometimes both may be involved. Thus, according to psychologist David Tiedeman and his colleagues, how realistic or efficient we are at making a decision often depends on how well we know ourselves and our environment.

Figure 2.1 graphically demonstrates how information affects our decisions over our lifetimes. As infants, we had no real control over what happened—all we could do was vocalize our discomfort while our parents tried to guess its source. As children, we learned more about ourselves and the world, and began to use two new strategies for decision making. If we didn't really know what we wanted to do, but knew about our environment, we were probably inclined to make dependent decisions. ("I'll get spanked if I don't do what Mommy says"; "I'd better do it her way.") If we knew what we wanted to do but were less certain about the conditions in the environment, we probably made *intuitive decisions* ("I don't want spinach. I want ice cream.") As we grew older, we retained the ability to make these two types of decisions, and added another strategy as well. That

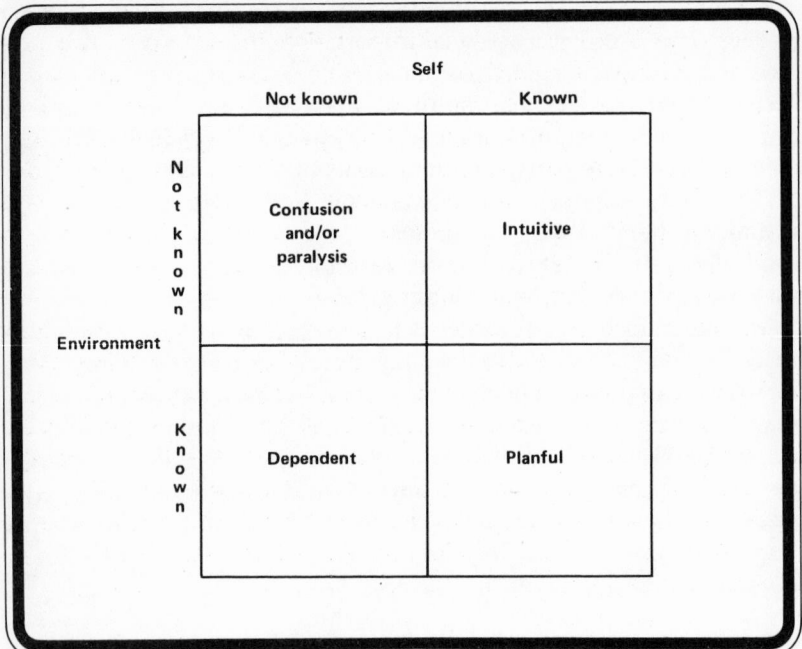

Figure 2.1 Learning decision strategies.

strategy, which we call a *planful decision*, takes into account both our knowledge of ourselves and the environment. When we use this strategy, we weigh the internal and external demands of the situation and the pros and cons (or costs and benefits) of the various alternatives we see. If there is time, we may gather and consider additional information about alternatives and possible consequences for both ourselves and our environment. The choices we make tend to fit our needs and our life situations better when we make planful decisions.

CHOOSING A STRATEGY

Since there are three alternative strategies for making a decision—and each has its own advantages and disadvantages—the first task in making a decision is to decide which strategy to use.

Dependent Decision Strategy

The *dependent decision* strategy may appear to be the easiest; we've certainly had the most time to practice it! All we need to do is defer the choice to others, to let someone else decide. In a situation where the outcome is of little personal importance, this approach can save time and energy. If you're like most of us, many of your dependent decisions are made in the spirit of compromise, as in the case of participating in a group decision. There are also situations that may call for a more informed dependent choice. If your doctor recommends surgery, for example, you may wish to get a second opinion or have the reasons carefully explained. Knowing that you don't have enough information to make the final decision, you may at least depend partially upon your doctor's judgment.

A dependent decision can be self-defeating and produce unhappy results if it is used to avoid the work of exploring or the fear making a choice on your own. Deferring a choice whose outcome is important out of fear or indecision does not help us to avoid the problem; it only means the decision will be out of our control, and will be made by others or by circumstances. The results will affect our lives just as if we had made the choice; even if we have transferred the decision elsewhere, the responsibility for coping with the results will still be ours.

Intuitive Decision Strategy

Decision makers who use the *intuitive decision* process rely on "gut-level" reactions; they check out their internal signals to see if something feels good. Intuitive decisions are usually made spontaneously and below one's level of awareness. Consequently, they take little time, data gathering, or conscious planning. They are useful in situations where time is at a premium, such as emergencies or unforeseen opportunities. Intuition often helps us in interpersonal relations, where factual data about the other person's reaction are not available. When used appropriately, intuition can help us retain both authority and responsibility in a difficut decision situation.

Intuitive decisions, however, can also have uncomfortable results if used as a substitute for or to avoid gathering needed information. In situations that are emotional or very important, intuitive hunches are sometimes hard to distinguish from wishful thinking or personal bias. If information and time to review a decision are available, it is usually wise to take advantage of them. After exploring, however, intuition or feelings may still play a part in the final decision. Intuition enjoys a better reputation now than in the past since we realize that hunches may really be perceptions based on information that is taken in over time but not consciously remembered. Nevertheless, it is probably wiser not to decide something on the basis of intuition alone, if there is other information available.

Planful Decision Strategy

The third strategy, the *planful decision* approach, involves exploration of our needs and the environment, and a rational weighing of the various alternatives, costs and benefits. The pace of this approach is slower than others, but allows maximum time for data gathering, exploring, and experimenting. Questions can be raised and answered, and attention paid to details. These questions will help us anticipate possible problems, and increase smoothness and efficiency of implementation. This approach does not exclude consideration of personal feelings about the choices (intuition) or the opinions of experts and loved ones (dependency), nor does it intend to exclude personal and idiosyncratic decision strategies.

Because the planful approach to decisions can consume a great deal of time and energy, it is not always appropriate. Many decisions are not important enough to be worth this amount of effort, and sometimes needed information is not available. Another problem is that in any situation the data are never all in, and waiting for everything we need to know can be a way of delaying a decision. Finally, anyone who takes this decision style literally runs the risk of making a totally rational or totally independent decision, which may not reflect reality, since our feelings and the opinions of significant others are important to us.

Ideally, a balanced decision will include elements of all three decision styles. Such a choice would consider information available from internal and external sources, weigh the validity of that information, and invest time in further exploration if it seems necessary. A productive decision will usually take into account whatever information one can marshall in the circumstances about self, others and the environment.

STAGES OF A PLANFUL CAREER DECISION

There are a number of ways to describe a planful career decision process. The decision stages that we have found most useful are summarized by the *decision cycle* shown in Figure 2.2.

① Awareness

This stage is usually heralded by a feeling of increasing discomfort in some area of our lives—an awareness of pressure for change. Unless we are willing to let the circumstances control us, we feel the necessity for making a decision. Sometimes such a need for decision is a happy and exciting leap into a new venture. Often, however, it is accompanied by doubts about the future and a desire to delay for fear of making a wrong choice, as well as a desire to act in spite of our lack of readiness. An important element of readiness lies in learning, examining, and refining our decision-making strategies. As we mentioned in Chapter 1, decision making is the first of five skills we must learn to plan our careers effectively.

If the changes that awareness may demand are very frightening, we sometimes postpone the decision until it is almost upon us. This may contribute to the sense of fear or even panic that sometimes accompanies awareness.

A major part of making the best decision in any situation is being sure that the problem is clearly defined before beginning the search for a solution. Sometimes we are so anxious to learn about alternatives that we fail to spend enough time sorting out the elements that comprise the problem. Examining the things that are blocking a decision can provide clues about where to look for help and what to do first. Understanding the problem requires referring to our own beliefs, attitudes and values, as well as those of our culture. Time

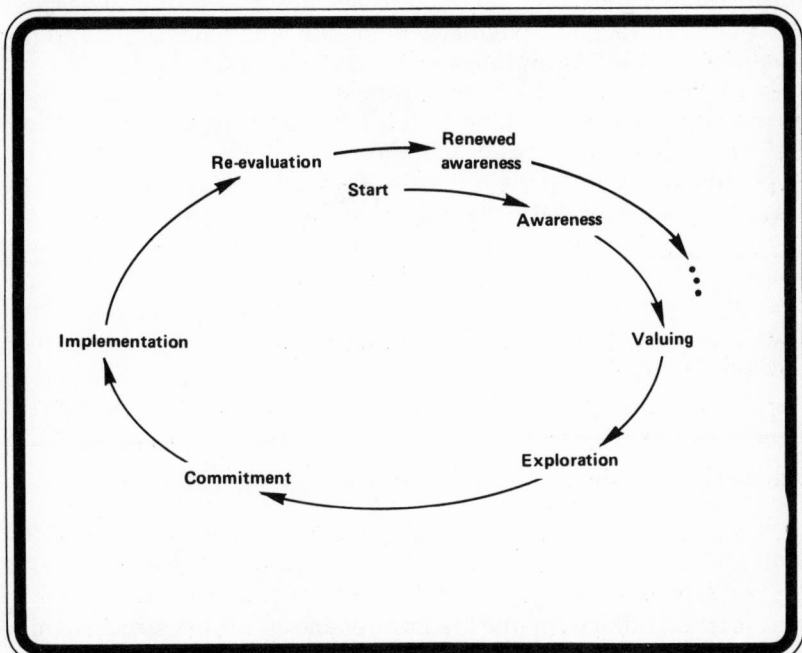

Figure 2.2 The decision cycle.

devoted to defining the problem may be well spent, particularly for those of us who feel confused by a multitude of options that they cannot organize or compare in any meaningful way. Confusion and anxiety can often be alleviated by pinpointing specific fears, irrational expectations, or skill and information deficits contributing to the problem.

② Valuing

As in defining the problem, the most valuable source of information for identifying desirable alternatives is ourselves. At this stage we begin to utilize the second of the five career-planning skills—self-assessment. Checking solutions against our beliefs, attitudes, and values can help us generate ways of dealing with situations that are consistent with our self-concepts. At this stage, in order to determine what we want and what we are willing to give up, time must be taken to determine the most valued outcomes of the decision. In short, the question to be answered is, "What do I most want to happen as an outcome of this decision?" Problems may occur at this stage if we are not really sure which outcome we most value. People who have made past decisions largely on a dependent or intuitive basis may not be fully aware of their own preferences and resources, or of what they are willing to sacrifice. Neither will people who have learned to put other people's wants and needs ahead of their own.

③ Exploration

The purpose of exploration is to make sure we have enough information about the situation and alternative ways of achieving the most desired outcomes. Career-planning skill number three involves learning needed strategies for gathering this occupational information; it can be integrated with the things we have learned about ourselves during the valuing stage. Based on relationships and discoveries synthesized from various kinds of information, alternatives can be generated for dealing with decision situations. It may be helpful to spend some time on each alternative, trying to think through the possible outcomes and how we would feel about them. As appealing alternatives are discovered, risks can be weighed, as well as the probability and cost of possible negative outcomes. After a number of realistic alternatives have been collected, deciding among these possible courses of action can be approached in two ways. We may start by eliminating the least acceptable alternatives and examine what is left, or we can start with the attractive ones and weigh each of them to identify the most practical and attainable one.

The process of exploring can be uncomfortable; it often creates confusion, conflict, and anxiety. The sheer amount of information available in many career areas increases the complexity of decision making, and presents new considerations or options that cause us to feel we must start over. Awareness of requirements and commitments involved in many choices can awaken fears of risk and failure. Such awareness can also bring the unwelcome realization that favored dreams and solutions may be blocked, or perhaps too difficult to be worthwhile. Although we can imagine ourselves as corporation presidents, we may find that we do not have the personal resources to strive to the corporate world's top levels.

People who have very many—or very few—areas of interest often discover several alternatives that appear to be equally attractive, but they have difficulty prioritizing them. Greater in-depth exploration, volunteer or trial work experience are several suggestions that may help differentiate interests, test abilities, and increase confidence. It may also help to review personal beliefs and goals.

Commitment

At some point you must choose one alternative to pursue, although others may be kept in reserve. Choosing one solution means eliminating others, at least temporarily, and sometimes permanently. This is hard to do; we are afraid we will be wrong and we hate to close off other options. Unfortunately, no single course of action can be pursued to its most successful conclusion if we are emotionally divided, or if we are spending energy trying to keep alternatives alive. The only way to discover if something will really work for us is to make a wholehearted commitment to it. Although some choices may be irreversible in the sense of time and personal resources spent, almost any decision can be reevaluated, altered, or abandoned at a later stage if we have the courage to look at it honestly.

Whether it is within ourselves or with others, personal conflict is a major factor that may block a decision at the commitment stage. People who really know what decision they want to make may nonetheless be stopped short by conflict with family or loved ones. Difficulties can be compounded by emotional or financial pressure, or by fear that the objections raised may prove to be right. The student who wants to be an electronics technician, for example, may find it difficult to buck a family tradition in dentistry. A second common kind of decision-blocking conflict is internal. Decision making in general causes anxiety for some of us, perhaps because past decisions have evoked criticism or unpleasant consequences.

⑤ Implementation

Once we have made a commitment, we implement our decision by initiating new courses of action or behaviors. We may gather information and start acquiring new skills or equipment. We may begin formal procedures for entering a training program or begin a job campaign. We may be able to change an old situation or create a new one using skills and opportunities that are already available. In all of these situations, we will need the fourth career-planning skill: ways of finding available jobs and of marketing ourselves. As we implement our decisions, we need to be aware of the feedback we are getting about the choice we have made. Does it fit our values? Have we done enough exploring? Have any of the circumstances changed?

If self-evaluation and exploration have been complete, any difficulties encountered in implementing a goal will not be a complete surprise. (Things do happen which cannot be foreseen or controlled, however, such as financial reversals, illness, or sudden changes in the environment.) Of course, hurdles and setbacks on the road to any goal—especially if it is a long one—may appear bigger or more discouraging in reality than they did in imagination, but that can often be remedied with a little rest or moral support. If, however, the pathway to implementation seems full of unpleasant surprises, exploration may have been incomplete or goals unrealistic.

Implementation of a chosen goal can still be blocked or delayed. An undergraduate aiming for graduate school may find that grades are not high enough, or that needed funds will not be available. A person whose decision seems permanently blocked may spend some time coping with disappointment before returning to the beginning of the decision cycle to search for attractive alternatives. In some cases, implementation of choices is simply delayed, and can only be successfully completed at a later time. People in such situations must wait, investigate other alternatives or alter dreams to fit their present circumstances.

⑥ Re-evaluation

After a decision is implemented, new behaviors are put into practice and life patterns altered. This stage of career development utilizes the final skill identified, work adjustment. Adjusting to a new work situation involves learning how to do tasks, and take and give direction while working cooperatively with other people. Keeping in tune with the job means finding out how to get new information, and learning new skills as they are needed.

After mastering the requirements of a new environment or role, an individual can begin to examine more closely whether it is fulfilling his or her expectations. If this course of action has not had the anticipated or desired results, the chooser may want to re-evaluate goals and alternatives. Possibilities to consider include:

1. The goal(s) are no longer appropriate or satisfying; they need to be revised.

2. Anticipated courses of action are no longer practical, or perhaps things are going so well they are not necessary.

3. Preferred alternatives that were previously unattainable may now be within reach.

New information and experiences need to be examined regularly to see if they have made a change in one's perspective or possibilities. Even if the initial choice has good results, circumstances may change or the situation may become monotonous because new challenges do not arise over a period of time. If unforeseen changes occur or hoped for changes fail to occur, awareness of a need for re-evaluation leads us back to the beginning of the decision cycle to go through each stage again. Even if we feel we know our present situation well, short-circuiting the decision process may keep us from discovering information that is essential to our next step. We may fail to re-evaluate decisions, thinking that we have the right answer that will work indefinitely. As we will be discussing later, fear of change may sometimes keep us from recognizing the need for re-evaluation, even when we are in a position that is beyond our capabilities.

The most important thing to remember about decision making and about what to look for in reviewing decisions is the inescapable nature of change: Everything changes. Our own beliefs, attitudes, and values will change. Our environment is changing with ever increasing rapidity. In 25 or even 5 years, many of our goals and skills will be obsolete. Even when we are in control of the externals, growth goes on within us long after we think we are grown-up. We can never be sure that any decision will be the right one at any time beyond the moment we make it. Our decisions and our world must grow and change with us.

DECISION STYLE WORKSHEET

Each of the boxes below contains a decision-making approach that you might use in making daily choices or important decisions. List three situations in each box that might prompt you to use the form of decision making represented in that box. Think of decisions you have made or discussed, or decisions made in such areas as family, friends, activities, classes, or jobs.

Three decisions that might cause me to become confused or paralyzed are:	Three decisions that I might let others make for me are:
1. _____	1. _____
2. _____	2. _____
3. _____	3. _____
Three decisions that I might make intuitively are:	Three decisions that I would be planful about are:
1. _____	1. _____
2. _____	2. _____
3. _____	3. _____

After you complete all four boxes, look back over the answers you wrote in each box. Do the situations in each box share anything in common? If they do, what is it?

How do the decisions you listed in each box differ from the decisions described in the other three boxes?

WHERE AM I IN THE CAREER DECISION-MAKING PROCESS?

Each of the boxes below contains a stage in the process of making a planful career decision. The goal or desired outcome of each stage is described and an example provided. Read through each of the stages and try to identify the stage where you are now in your own career decision making. After you have identified that stage, write in the spaces provided what you will have to do to move you to the next stage and each of the stages that follow. When you complete this activity for your own plans, you may wish to use the vignettes in Appendix A to further sharpen your decision-making skills. Each vignette presents a person who is attempting to make a career decision. Try to formulate a planful decision-making approach for that individual.

Awareness

Goal: To clearly define the decision you need to make.

Example: I need to decide on an academic major at the end of this term.

The decision I need to make is:

Valuing

Goal: To decide how important the decision is to you, what you want to accomplish by it, and what effort or sacrifice you are willing to make to achieve it.

Example: My decision about an academic major is very important to me. I want to go to law school and I need to major in an area that will most help me get into law school. I need to make this decision by the end of this term so I can graduate on schedule.

What I want to accomplish by this decision is:

Exploration

Goal: To identify and explore at least two possible courses of action.

Example: I'll explore political science and psychology since both are applicable to law. I'll take three weeks to explore both fields by reading about them in the *Occupational Outlook Handbook* and professional literature, talking to people in both fields, and talking to academic advisors in each area. Before I do, I'll make a checks and balances sheet about each field. This will allow me to compare them with each other in terms of things that I like and don't like about each.

Two areas that I want to explore are:
1.

2.

The ways that I will explore them are:

1. _____

2. _____

3. _____

4. _____

I will complete my exploration by _____
(date)

Commitment

Goal: To make a choice of one alternative and inform others about it.

Example: I've decided on political science. I'll tell my academic advisor about my decision; I'll inform my family as well since they are interested in what I do. I'll let them know about my decision in four weeks.

I've decided to:

The person(s) I want to inform about my decision are:

1. _____

2. _____

3. _____

I will inform all of them by _____
                                              (date)

Implementation

Goal: To act on your decision.

Example: After I talk to my advisor and get his or her suggestions about which political science classes to take, I'll enroll for them at preregistration for next term.

The actions I need to take to implement my decision are:

1. _____

2. _____

3. _____

4. _____

5. _____

Re-evaluation

Goal: After you have lived with your choice for a reasonable length of time, you'll review it and, if necessary, identify new choices to be made.

Example: At the end of the next term, I'll spend some time reviewing how I feel about political science. If I'm uncomfortable with it as a choice, I'll identify what it is about it that makes me uncomfortable and look at other possible majors that may be more consistent with what I like to do.

I'll re-evaluate my decision by _____.
                                                                (date)

When I do so, I'll make my judgment using the following criteria:

1. _____

2. _____

3. _____

REFERENCES

GeLatt, H. B., Varenhorst, B., Carey, R., and Miller, G. P. *Decisions and Outcomes*, New York: College Entrance Examination Board, 1973.

O'Neil, N. and O'Neil, G. *Shifting Gears: Finding Security in a Changing World*, New York: M. Evans and Co., Inc., 1974.

Tiedeman, D. V. and O'Hara, R. P. *Career Development: Choice and Adjustment*, New York: College Entrance Examination Board, 1963.

chapter

3

The Emerging Self: Birth to Adolescence

Sow an act and reap a habit;
Sow a habit and reap a character;
Sow a character and reap a destiny.

Boardman

It is a special morning. Snow from the distant mountains has come down to blanket the houses and frost the trees. Inside, nine-year-old Sarah is helping with breakfast. John, age ten, is outside shoveling the walk with his dad. After breakfast Sarah opens the biggest present under the tree—a beautiful doll. Four-year-old Jimmy wails with envy and reaches for it. Mommy hands him a shiny new truck. Jimmy wonders why he cannot have a doll.

Jerry sits in biology class, staring out the window. He is Uncle Harry's favorite nephew, and the family has always assumed he will become a doctor and share his uncle's practice. He tried to tell his dad he likes auto mechanics and shop better than science, but his dad tells him he can do those things as hobbies—he will have plenty of time once the money starts rolling in from his medical practice. Besides, he is not sure he wants to go to college right now. Several of his friends joined the Navy, and they look great in their uniforms. They are traveling around, meeting girls and making their own decisions. Jerry thinks maybe, if he did that for a while, he could figure out some things about himself.

Each moment, people of all shapes, ages, and backgrounds struggle with the timeless question, "Who am I?" They are going through a time of change, discovering that they no longer fit comfortably in their skins or situations, and that something must go—or grow. Old decisions and commitments once seen as permanent may need to be reviewed. New situations may occur in which old behaviors and solutions do not work anymore, and new ones must therefore be created.

Choices about a career are among the most major and far-reaching decisions of our lives. They also present the greatest challanges and cause the strongest feelings of not being able to turn back again. The expression of ourselves through work fills not only a large part of each day, but many of our needs as well. Consequently, any larger changes in who we are, how we see ourselves, or how we live, significantly affect ourselves vocationally.

YOU ARE A PERSON WHO . . .

Although no one is certain exactly how they operate, processes that define and redefine an individual's total self-concept—including the vocational part of it—begin at birth. From the start, our physical appearances, capabilities, limitations, or problems immediately began to affect the way we coped with our environment and the kind of feedback we got from it. Our early attempts to influence our surroundings were instinctive, and our success—or lack of it—influenced our sense of competency from life's first months. The kind of responses we got to our crying, laughter, and first tentative words determined our basic attitudes about ourselves and our relationship to our environment.

The most critical influences on our personal development were largely social and cultural. In infancy and early childhood, for example, we learned that we were acceptable when we smiled, walked, talked, became toilet trained, and dressed ourselves. We imitated older siblings and adults (especially those of the same gender), and soon adopted family beliefs and family ways of expressing attitudes about work, love, religion, and loved ones. Because we learned these beliefs and values at such an early age and in such subtle ways, we are often not aware of them or of how we acquired them. Nonetheless, by age three or four, many of these expectations, especially those associated with gender, were firmly established in our minds.

In school, we rapidly learned that study was the order of the day and recess a treat to be earned through successful work. The work ethic thus began to influence us early in our lives. And, whether or not our mothers stayed at home, an important prejudice was passed on to many of us—the implicit idea that real work is associated with being away from home, and with external reinforcements such as grades or money. During this time, and into our early adolescent years, fantasy role tryouts also played an important part in our vocational development. Many of our vocational role models came from storybooks or TV; we dressed up and played at being parents, teachers, nurses, or sports heroes.

WHO AM I?

At adolescence we were expected to start looking ahead; to think about how we would choose to live and to support ourselves after high school or college. Sometimes, the decision was predetermined. Perhaps we had one outstanding talent or interest that we pursued with dedication. Or, we might have had a family business or parental occupation which we were expected to and wanted to train for. For others of us, adolescence heralded the beginning of a struggle to be free from family directives and to "do our own thing," or to do what our peers were doing. A mass of choices lay ahead, offering new opportunities for self-discovery. At the same time that we saw our horizons expanding, we were met with the demand that a career (or at least an educational objective) be declared. Fantasy gave way to confusion and exploration. Even if we did not know what we wanted to do, we felt we had to do something and we wanted it to be the right thing. Consequently, we struggled to establish new external and internal guidelines for our thoughts, feelings and actions. We began to explore our own interests and we tested ourselves to discover our capabilities. We may have become intensely involved with one activity or friend and when that no longer fit, we moved on. We tried out various clubs, hobbies, jobs, classes, attitudes, roles, and relationships. Gradually, we developed a relatively stable pattern of interests and values, and began to base our decisions on them.

For many of us, especially those who grew up prior to the 1970's, social stereotypes often operated unchallenged in high school. We may have unwittingly established friendships along racial or socioeconomic lines. Sex role stereotypes also had a special influence at that time because relationships between the sexes had a new, confusing, and urgent role in our lives. In our society boys have traditionally been expected to assume leadership roles, develop mechanical, analytical, and mathematical abilities, and develop physical prowess in sports. As a consequence, boys have tended to take on these roles with little thought of what they were doing. More often, girls have been taught to take on complementary roles. They concentrated on relationships, developed verbal and artistic skills, and sometimes became, literally and figuratively, cheerleaders for the males' accomplishments. These divisions were most often reinforced by teachers, peers, and families, who said that these were realities of the work environment.

Because we admired and depended on adults as children, we have probably carried many of their beliefs and attitudes into adulthood—sometimes without examining them in the light of our own experience. The result is that many of us have blind spots or prejudices. We see our own abilities and vocational opportunities—or those of others—as being limited by factors that may not be relevant, such as sex, race, or age. Sometimes, because of such childhood learning, we may believe we cannot do, or are not interested in, things we have never tried. This is a new era, however, and supportive groups and resources are now available in many communities and schools to encourage work role experimentation. Women can take shop or auto mechanics, or get help with anxiety over math. Men can take courses in parenting or gourmet cooking. Boys find that they can enjoy being expressive and supportive, and girls find leadership roles available and assertiveness rewarding.

We may choose to keep some of our old beliefs or to change them. The important thing is that we have the freedom and responsibility to examine our values and make our own decisions. Recent legislation and increased awareness of these stereotypes are changing attitudes and opportunities, both in the schools and in the job market, and we as individuals are challenging these old rules. Equal employment opportunity legislation is aimed at encouraging the hiring of people who want to work at jobs not traditionally available to them. We now see increasing numbers of male nurses and homemakers, female engineers and doctors, and black lawyers and business executives. Examining stereotypes that we hold about ourselves and others can open up new perspectives about careers, our lifestyles, and ourselves.

I AM A PERSON WHO . . .

In young adulthood the pressure is really on us to make decisions and carry them out! The cute question, "What are you going to be when you grow up?" is not funny anymore. It is an imperative. We are expected to make choices for ourselves, but we may not feel ready. People at this age have many ways of coping with this threatening freedom. Some people are challenged and excited by it, some try to avoid it, and some keep their options open and perhaps make tentative commitments.

Separating oneself from the family, physically and emotionally, is the primary goal of this age span. A balance must be achieved between our desires for autonomy and dependence upon others. Driving means freedom, but often only with permission to use the family car. College often means living away from home and the pleasures of self-direction, but these freedoms may conflict with continued dependence on family money. As emerging adults, we spend our energies gaining control over our own lives and learning to make decisions. The emotional isolation and responsibility for our own lives that comes with young adulthood can be lonely and confusing. We socialize and "party" in an effort to learn what emotional and sexual options are available, how these things fit our values and attitudes, and how to implement our choices. The family no longer meets all of our emotional needs, yet we may lack the skills and courage to start building an emotional support system on our own. This gap may be filled by school friends or roommates, fraternities and clubs, a premarriage or marriage commitment, or an organization such as a religious group or the military. The choices we make about how we will meet our personal needs help to shape our life-style. We consider whether we want to be married or single, parents or not, conservatives or swingers. We begin to get ideas about where we might want to work, what hours, and with what kind of people. Such decisions about life-style can be joyous and exciting, but if these commitments are made in the fear of freedom, they can be ways of handing our life decisions to someone else to handle. For some, occupational or life decisions come easy; others may remain confused or choose goals in haste to escape uncertainty. It takes courage to choose to remain confused, but if those of us who have not decided can keep our minds open to new information about the world and ourselves, we will eventually begin to identify avocational and vocational activities that represent a comfortable combination of what we want and what we perceive as possible and acceptable. The building blocks of dealing with the tasks of adulthood can be shaped and fit together to form our vocational self-concept. The balance of all the pieces will never be ideal, and will require periodic adjustment as we develop and continue to perceive new opportunities.

These pieces of our vocational selves are identified in Table 3.1 in terms of when we most likely acquired them, what they are, and how they influence our careers. Table 3.1 also indicates where in this text the various parts of our vocational selves are discussed.

As is shown in Table 3.1, the hallmark of childhood was that we accepted what others told us to believe about ourselves and the world around us. We used fantasy to project our ideal vocational self-images, and developed an emerging awareness of how best to balance our time and energies. Adolescence was marked by questioning, exploring, and sometimes challenging old standards to realistically assess ourselves. With experience, preferences about work gave way to a more realistic assessment of our interests and skills. In young adulthood, the urge to become one's own person, to become autonomous, leads us to clarify what we value and want and how we will work to get it.

As we begin to know and understand ourselves, we need a way of organizing our self-knowledge and of determining how our personal qualities fit into the world of work. Based upon its surveys of worker characteristics and work tasks, the U.S. Department of Labor suggests that our personal and vocational characteristics tend to pull together and seek expression in three interacting spheres of activity as illustrated in Figure 3-1 (p. 55).

The overlapping of the spheres in Figure 3-1 acknowledges that individual variations on the Data/Ideas–People–Things dimensions are really best understood in "more than/less than" terms. Because we possess the basic endowment and life opportunities to develop a variety of abilities, we may have skills in all three areas but tend to prefer work activities in only one or two. Avocational activities

TABLE 3.1

Factors Affecting Our Vocational Self-Concepts

When	What	Influence on your career
Childhood	Your *energy level* is the amount of physical and mental energy you have, and influences the amount of energy you wish to invest in each of your daily pursuits, including your work and leisure activities.	As we will be exploring here, and in Chapters 5 and 6, your energy level is affected by your heredity, diet, patterns of activity and rest, age, and health. Since your energy level influences the amount and intensity of your activities, it will shape the level and types of responsibilities you pursue at work, the amount of stress you can handle, and the amount of physical and mental exertion you can invest in work and leisure tasks (your lifestyle).
	Your *attitudes and beliefs* are your subjective views of the world around you; the way you expect things to be and believe they "should" be, the way you perceive and form opinions about things.	The activity, "Removing additudinal blocks to career decision making", pointed out how your attitudes and beliefs can have a positive or negative effect on the way you view yourself and your work. Decisions based on unrealistic, incomplete, or outdated beliefs may lead you to restrict your options or to undertake too much, and can result in disappointment with your career(s).
	Your *aspirations* are the things you fantasize or dream about doing soon or someday.	As was noted earlier in this chapter, during childhood most of us saw work in idealized ways. We dreamed of being somebody special and often played at being persons of high status or prominence, largely because of the uniform they wore, their ability to influence others, or the excitement of their jobs. Whether or not you live out your childhood dreams depends largely upon the

talents you possess, the opportunities you have to develop them, and the time and energy you invest in realizing them. In the chapters that follow, we will explore how the balance between your dreams and the realities of what you can actually achieve may affect the views you have of yourself as an adult and the levels and kinds of work at which you can be most successful.

As we gain in life experience and are exposed to more information about the world of work, our fantasies give way to preferences and our mental self-portraits become clearer. We can identify occupations that appeal to us but also recognize that we may not have the capabilities to be successful at all of them. As will become clearer in Chapter 5, understanding what your most preferred occupations share in common can help you identify the personal skills and interest areas you would like to develop, and majors and occupations for exploration. Since our interests reflect the direct experiences we have had with different occupationally related activities, they tend to become more stable as we get older. Occupational interest surveys can be used to compare our interests with those of persons who are successful and satisfied in a variety of occupations. Such comparisons can help you identify occupational areas that employ persons who have interests that are similar to yours. They also provide you with an idea of how you would have to reshape your interests in order to enter and enjoy occupations that employ persons whose interests are dissimilar to yours. One such survey is found in Appendix A.

Your *preferences* are what you would like to do if reality would permit.

Your *interests* are more realistic than your preferences; they reflect the experiences or ideas you have had about work-related activities that you like or dislike.

Adolescence

TABLE 3.1 (*continued*)

Factors Affecting Our Vocational Self-Concepts

When	What	Influence on your career
Adolescence	Your *skills* or abilities are the things you can do; they help you define the level on which you could operate within various areas of interest.	Like our interests, our skills reflect the experiences we have had with work-related activities, especially those that require particular ways of thinking, moving, or relating to others to achieve a goal or to produce a product. Like interests, your skills can be measured and compared with the skill requirements of different professions and academic areas. Skills can be transferred to and implemented in many different interest areas. Thus it is important to identify skills and to separate them from interest in your mind. The survey found in Appendix A will allow you to compare your skills with persons in different curricular areas. Chapter 5 will help you explore how your skills and interests can be tied into different occupations.
Adulthood	Your *values* are what you are for or against, what is important to you and in what order. They determine what you want from your life.	Since our values reflect the things that we cherish or prize, they help us judge the appropriateness of specific work activities for us, and the importance we place on work in comparison to homelife and leisure pursuits. An inventory that will help you identify and explore how your values have emerged and changed over time and what you currently value is provided at the end of the next chapter.

may balance these three areas or provide outlets for interests and skills not tapped in the work setting.

Generally speaking, an individual who is oriented and skilled at working with "people" enjoys involvements with others and prefers interpersonal situations that allow opportunities to lead, persuade, teach, or counsel. The individual with interests and competencies that are more strongly focused on the "data/ideas" dimension tends to enjoy working with numbers and abstract concepts expressed through words and symbols. As the name implies, an individual with a "things" orientation likes working with machinery, tools, and instruments and enjoys problem solving in real physical situations.

John Holland has extended the Data/Ideas–People–Things framework while retaining much of its simple practicality. His studies have led him to conclude that within each of the Data/Ideas–People–Things spheres there are two dimensions. He suggests that there are six general work personality types. These personality types are briefly described in Figure 3.2. Titles and activities that are associated with each of these personality types are also described in this figure.

Types that are on the adjacent corners of the hexagon are said to

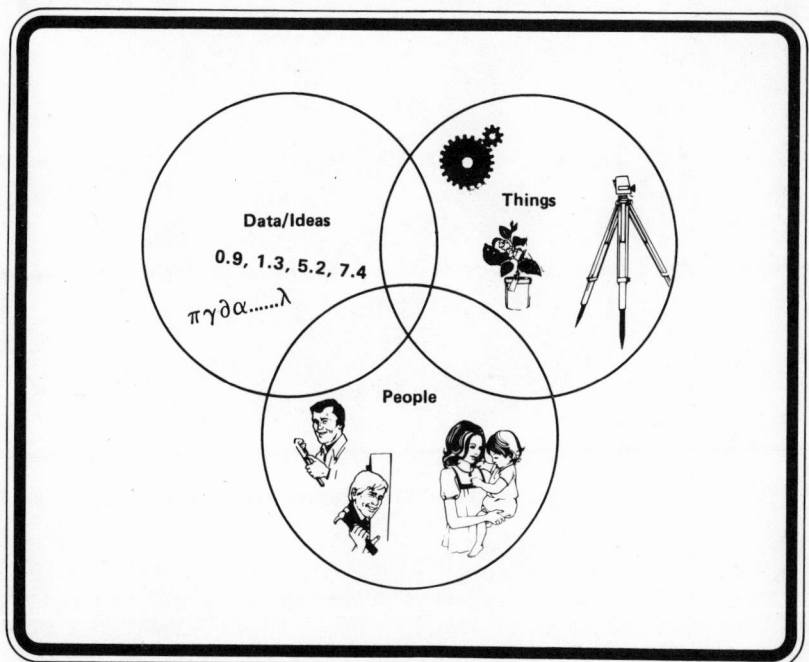

Figure 3.1 *Spheres of work activity.*

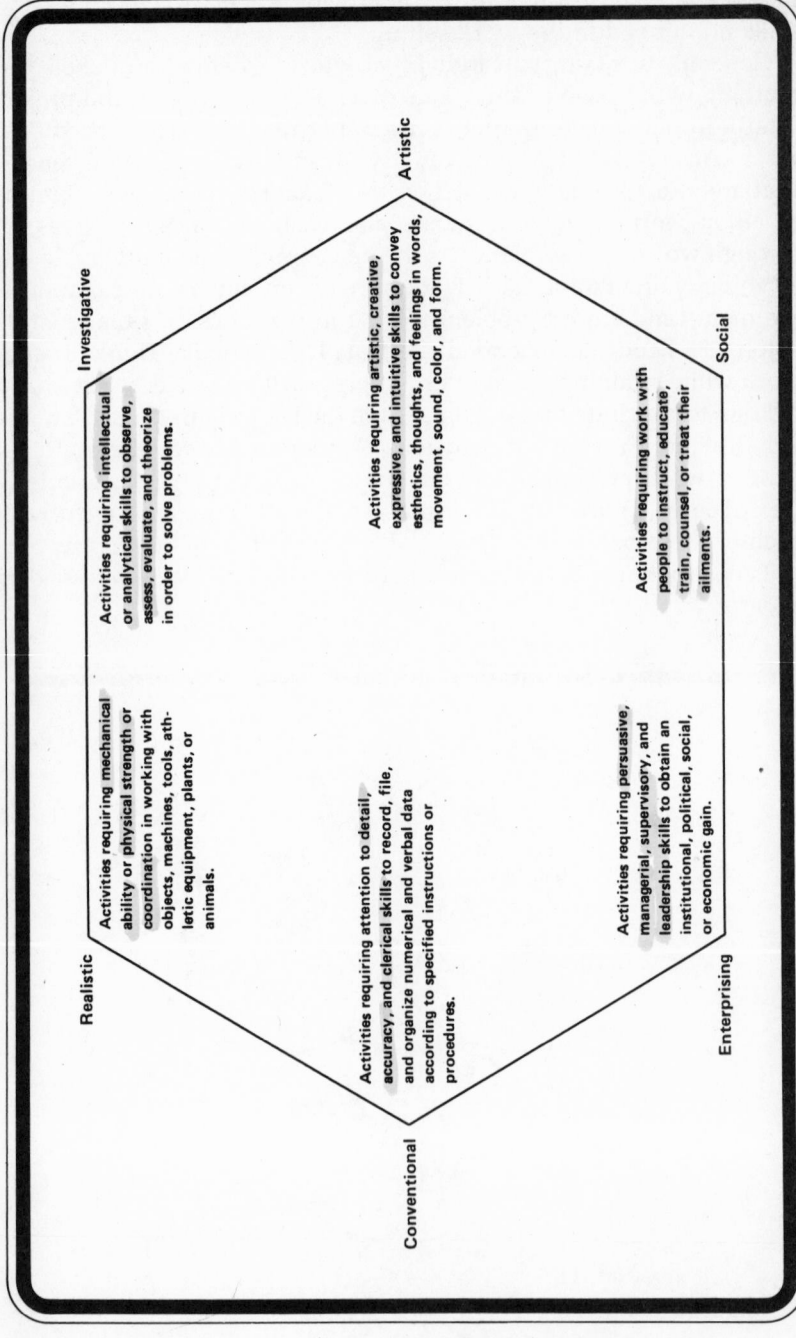

Realistic
Activities requiring mechanical ability or physical strength or coordination in working with objects, machines, tools, athletic equipment, plants, or animals.

Investigative
Activities requiring intellectual or analytical skills to observe, assess, evaluate, and theorize in order to solve problems.

Artistic
Activities requiring artistic, creative, expressive, and intuitive skills to convey esthetics, thoughts, and feelings in words, movement, sound, color, and form.

Social
Activities requiring work with people to instruct, educate, train, counsel, or treat their ailments.

Enterprising
Activities requiring persuasive, managerial, supervisory, and leadership skills to obtain an institutional, political, social, or economic gain.

Conventional
Activities requiring attention to detail, accuracy, and clerical skills to record, file, and organize numerical and verbal data according to specified instructions or procedures.

Figure 3.2 John Holland's Worker Traits—Work Activities Hexagon.

be consistent. That is, the closer two types are on the hexagon, the more psychologically similar they are. So, if you have Realistic characteristics, you are more likely to exhibit a personality pattern that shares Conventional and Investigative interests, skills, and values. If your orientation is more Social, you may have some Artistic and Enterprising qualities. Since types can "compete" within one person, you may have difficulty determining a preferred occupational direction if you related to several types with equal intensity, or are oriented toward types located at opposite points of the hexagon.

After examining the six personality types, most people agree that they possess characteristics associated with all corners of the hexagon. However, specific corners are probably more representative than others. By rank ordering the six types, you may begin to explore the kinds of work activities that interest you. The three that you rank highest may provide clues about work activities that you like and serve as an aid in determining occupational directions for you to explore.

ACTIVITY

Carefully read through each of the six descriptions below. After you do, rank order the six types of activity, starting with the one that is most like you and ending with the one that is least like you. Write "1" on the line beside the type that is most like you, "2" beside the one that is next most like you, and so on until you have put a number beside all of the six types.

Ranking   *Types*

_____   Realistic: Activities requiring mechanical ability, physical strength, or coordination in working with objects, machines, tools, athletic equipment, plants, or animals.

_____   Investigative: Activities requiring intellectual or analytical skills to observe, assess, evaluate, and theorize in order to solve problems.

_____   Artistic: Activities requiring artistic, creative, expressive, and intuitive skills to convey esthetics, thoughts, and feelings in words, movement, sound, color, and form.

_____   Social: Activities requiring work with people to instruct, educate, train, counsel, or treat their ailments.

_____   Enterprising: Activities requiring persuasive, managerial, supervisory, and leadership skills to obtain an institutional, political–social, or economic gain.

_____   Conventional: Activities requiring attention to detail, accuracy, and clerical skills to record, file, and organize numerical and verbal data according to specified instructions or procedures.

In ranking the six types of activity above, you have in a way predicted the outcome of any interest or abilities inventory that you might take which uses Holland's Worker Types as its format. One inventory that uses Holland's approach is provided in Appendix B of this book. Turn to it now and complete it to get a sense of how well your predictions about yourself compare with your inventoried interests and abilities.

REFERENCES

Crites, J. O. *Vocational Psychology*, New York: McGraw-Hill, 1969.

Holland, J. L. *Making Vocational Choices: A Theory of Careers*, Englewood Cliffs, New Jersey: Prentice-Hall, 1973, pp. 12–13.

Matteson, D. R. *Adolescence Today: Sex Roles and The Search for Identity*. Homewood, Illinois: The Dorsey Press, 1975.

The Emerging Self: Beyond Adolescence

Coming and Going

i have noticed
that men
somewhere around forty
tend to come in from the field
with a sigh
and removing their coat in the hall
call into the kitchen

> you were right
> grace
> it ain't out there
> just like you've always said

and she
with the children gone at last
breathless
puts her hat on her head

> the hell it ain't

coming and going
they pass
in the doorway   Ric Masten

It's two o'clock on an autumn afternoon. Bill sits at his window and watches a squirrel gathering nuts for a bitter east coast winter—he retired the previous June. The first few months were full of freedom and fun, like a vacation. Now free time, so precious during those working years, is becoming a burden to Bill. There's nothing to plan or rest up for; no tasks whose value to others can be measured by a paycheck. Friends that Bill planned to lunch or fish with during these "sunset years" have moved to warmer climates, or passed on. He's not really a parent anymore—his children are parents themselves. For the first time in many years, Bill is uncertain about what he wants from the rest of his life.

Sara sits on her front steps as her children play. She concentrates on how lucky she is, mentally listing her nice home, healthy children, and adoring husband. She has gotten a part-time job as a receptionist at a mental health center—a lucky break for someone with an associate degree in psychology and no experience. The people Sara works with have encouraged her to go back to school; she and Joe have talked about rearranging child and household responsibilities so that she can. Sara knows it will take a lot of time and energy, but she has decided to try it.

The pressure is on very early in this society to grow up, become mature, be adults. We are supposed to sort out our values, choose a vocation, a way of living and then settle down. The implication is that, if we make the right choices, we will be safe—home free for the rest of our lives. Children are expected to grow, change, make mistakes and modify themselves. But once we reach adulthood we are supposed to be serene, sure, and stable. Adults don't get confused, act foolish, evade reality, or feel dependent. Or do they?

The myth of adulthood is that if we do what we are supposed to do (regardless of whether we *want* to), we will achieve certain outcomes. This is what George and Nina O'Neill (1974) call "the maturity myth." We are tacitly promised by our culture that if we follow the rules, these results are guaranteed:

1. We will be home safe when we reach our forties.
2. We will be stable and not restless.
3. We will have emotional security.
4. The future will be manageable.

The major problem with these guarantees is that they might come true. It is not very likely since no one can foresee or guarantee our future, let alone its quality. But if they should come true, each has its negative corollary:

1. When you are living safely there will be no new directions, nothing to anticipate but old age.
2. When you are less restless, you will be less curious and your life will be repetitive.
3. The more you expect emotional security, the more threatening change will be—and change is unavoidable.
4. If it is totally manageable, your future will be without challenge or excitement.

ADULT LIFE STAGES

To the extent that these promises come true, you will stop growing and changing, and that only happens when we are dead. As Germaine Greer succinctly puts it: "Security is when everything is settled, when nothing can happen to you. Security is a denial of life."

Researchers on adult development are finding more and more evidence of an orderly series of adult stages and transitions through which we will change and grow as long as we live. As scary as this may seem, it takes the pressure off. We no longer have to have it all together, or make all our decisions by a certain age. We no longer have to pretend to others, ourselves, or our children that we are faultless. We can take our confusions and problems out from under wraps. Maturity is not a goal but a growth process. However, it appears to be hard for us to win permission from ourselves and our society to grow, experiment, and change. The psychiatrist, Roger Gould, attributes this to the magical expectations of adulthood and adults that we learn as children—the "maturity myth." He believes that we are in for minimal growth and maximal misery as adults unless we confront the realities of adulthood, and stop expecting that we should be perfect and have all the answers.

Growth circles back upon itself; change is both the impetus for growth and its product. Change is where career decisions—as all major decisions—begin and end. It is both exciting and frightening, and we can depend on it to be unavoidable. Change often travels with crisis; in part, this has to do with timing. Sometimes change comes when we are not ready for it, such as a personal loss or a job that is phased out. Or, we may be ready for a change that does not come: a promotion, a raise, or some new friends. Even when a change is well timed, it involves an act of faith, letting go of the familiar to embrace the unknown. Part of learning to cope with change is to believe in growth, to put aside fear and frustration long enough to realize that change is a catalyst for transition. Everything around us is growing; if we try to stand still we will not avoid change, we will simply be giving up our option to choose and to help direct it. A crisis is often the chance for a ride to the next stage of our development. Not a free ride, but often, in terms of experience, a real bargain.

Adult life stages appear to be ordered, each one must be completed before the next one can be genuinely undertaken. There is a great temptation (and sometimes pressure) to jump ahead. Time and competition are important to Americans. Sometimes we are so anxious to go forward that stopping to sort out and tie up loose ends seems like wasted time, but there are no shortcuts. Like infants, we must crawl before we can walk. A person who tries to circumvent growth phases by leaping forward to keep up with the expectations of a parent, employer, or spouse is setting the stage for serious trouble for him or herself and for that relationship.

Each person's existence is guided by internal beliefs and external demands. It is much easier to see and understand the external elements. Our social, family, and job roles are filled with things we perceive to be controlling us: I should do this, I have to do that, I can't do something else. We often define our lives in terms of external success and others' opinions, and we may be tempted to blame failures and distress on spouses, jobs and society's problems. We may try to define the appropriateness of our attitudes and values according to external events and expectations, and when or if the two do not mesh, we blame ourselves. Looking inward is the *first* place we need to look to find our own direction, not the last. Which of these things is for me? How do I feel about each of them? Although crises and growth experiences may be altered by and attuned to our environment, they frequently begin and end inside us.

Each life stage has its own implications for all the decisions we make: for our work, personal selves and life-styles. In general, the discoveries made about adult development have triggered the realization that a career choice usually becomes a series of choices. As the environment changes, our internal landscape is changing as well. As we gain new life experiences, our values, interests, feelings, and even our capacities may shift. If it is to be fulfilling, our career may need to be re-evaluated, too.

Early Adulthood (Ages 20 to 30)

In our early twenties (or sooner) we face a conflict between the desire for stability and the desire to explore. At this age we are expected to start making commitments to a life system of our own. For many postadolescents this push to commitment comes when there are still too many loose ends. Young adults respond to this confusion in many ways. Some continue to explore different sets of values and attitudes by experimenting with various kinds of living arrangements and temporary jobs. Many young adults, however, appear to turn their backs on unexplored horizons and begin working to establish themselves. Some of these people may have sorted out what they want and feel ready to settle down. For others, a career choice and/or marriage may be seen as the right path to adulthood and security. For them the misfortune is not in the doing, but in the fact that many people believe that deciding simply to decide will guarantee happiness—again, the "maturity myth."

In other words, society traditionally told us that our 20's are the decade when we should start a family and establish a permanent career direction. Recently, however, more and more people are successfully trying other options. Women are marrying later and filling more professional and executive level jobs. Increasingly numbers of couples are combining two careers with parenthood or choosing not to have children. Numerous homemakers and workers of both sexes beyond their 20's are returning to school or work to launch second (or third or fourth) careers. In effect, as social change occurs, many people are changing their attitudes and life-styles. Some are forced to change by loss of a job or spouse; others are choosing change in order to take advantage of new opportunities. Thus, making a commitment during the 20's, which later turns out to be uncomfortable, need not be a devastating mistake. In fact, research seems to indicate that those who commit themselves wholeheartedly to something in this stage—even if they outgrow it—are better equipped for much of the growth that occurs later in life.

One important outgrowth of commitment to any endeavor is the opportunity to learn from more experienced colleagues in the work setting. Many researchers on adult development agree that one valuable kind of learning experience during the 20's and 30's, especially important in developing a career, is a relationship with a mentor.

A *mentor* is someone who is far enough along in his or her own emotional and career development to guide and help younger workers. The mentor has more experience than younger colleagues have and is usually at a higher occupational level. He or she can provide an informal source of information, influence and support. This is the way most unexperienced workers refine their skills and learn shortcuts, informal (often unspoken) rules, and processes in a particular business environment or career area.

He or she can be a boss or a co-worker, or someone outside the immediate work environment, even in a different career area. Although mentors are most often of the same sex, cross-gender relationships are becoming increasingly common. This is especially significant for women, who may need the informal tutoring and sponsorship of a mentor but have had difficulty finding one. This was due in the past to the lack of females at the higher levels of many work environments, and to the hesitation of many males to mentor a female (due to kidding from other males or sexual overtones). The situation is now changing, and most people, during the years their careers and skills are developing, will have several mentors as they change jobs or advance within a field.

Re-examination (Ages 30 to 40)

No matter how settled the 20's may have seemed, the pathway into the 30's may involve a reappearance of some of the confusion and self-doubts that we put aside, or thought we solved, in adolescence. There may be conflict in this stage between obligations we have taken on and unfulfilled personal desires. We begin to understand that some of our "shoulds" were accepted from our families and society, and we ask, "Why *should* I?" We begin to realize that the rewards we expected for doing what we were told may not be forthcoming. We may think of rearranging our obligations in order to realize our hopes and dreams. At 35, according to U.S. life expectancy tables, we have lived half our lives. It is around this age that many of us begin to feel pressed for time. These feelings of lost opportunity, combined with the prospect of middle and old age ahead, create a feeling of urgency that Gail Sheehy has called the "last chance" syndrome. We feel that if we miss the opportunity to do what we really want to do now it will be too late. This feeling often impels people at this stage to reexamine and reevaluate personal values and attitudes, as well as their career progress and goals. In doing so, we may find that some of our beliefs and goals are no longer attainable or appropriate. Many people in their mid-30's today find that values and attitudes about basic things like work, sex and marriage, family structure, and sex roles are now radically different from the traditions that they grew up with. A study done by Daniel Yankelovich in 1978 indicates that the old motivations—money, security and status—no longer have meaning for many of today's workers. The majority of the workers Yankelovich interviewed said that leisure is their major source of satisfaction, not work. Workers today seem to feel they have a right to a secure living, and that the most important rewards of their job are increased independence and self-fulfillment. Many workers, especially women, value a paycheck as a recognition of their contributions as an individual.

If we are to be comfortable in our culture, our attitudes and expectations must change in relation to the changing demands of reality, as well as changing attitudes. One result of the American worker's increasing affluence, mobility, and quest for self-fulfillment is a new attitude toward job change. Many of us have a parent (or grandparent) who was a loyal employee of one firm for 30 or 40 years, and retired with a ceremony and a gold watch. Now, the average worker may change jobs several times during his or her career and may retrain at some point to enter a partially or entirely different area. Additional changes we face include growing competition for jobs, changes made by changing social attitudes and legislation, and a growing number of jobs that are becoming overcrowded or obsolete. Although we often cannot foresee these changes when we are training ourselves for a first career, we can stay alert for change by keeping our learning and decision skills sharp, and by observing our surroundings and maintaining our flexibility.

Over our working lives many kinds of changes can occur. In addition to a job shift—being fired, laid off, quitting, taking a new job, or even starting a whole new career—changes are common within one company or enterprise, or even within a job. These include: promotion, demotion, shifts in job duties, a leave of absence, a transfer to a new location, a change of income, additional school or on-the-job retraining, the loss of employees, bosses or colleagues, or even something as subtle as a change in your feelings about your job. The late 30's is the time when many workers leave their last mentor relationship, strike out to form their own power base, and perhaps prepare to become a mentor for someone else. Whether we view these changes as good or bad, they will require adjustments and decisions on our part, and will affect our present and future feelings and behaviors. Single workers may find that such changes affect friends, roommates, dates, or parents. Career-related events in the lives of married workers will affect the spouse (and any other family members). Dual-career marriages present special problems, including that of finding a location where both spouses may pursue their career interests. The feelings and the household routines of husbands and children can present problems for a wife who wants to begin working, or for a woman who wants to have a family while continuing to work. These effects on other people who may be in our lives—spouses, children, parents, or friends—will be important considerations for most of us. A man who gets a job offer in a new city may want to involve his family in the decision, especially if his children are involved in the community, or if his wife has a career outside the home. If either spouse wishes to invest time and money in school or retraining, this may involve asking others to cut their standard of living or assume new responsibilities. Women in their 30's today are being affected by inflation, by divorce or widowhood, by social attitudes, and by the realization that the job of motherhood only fills 10 to 20 of their 40 (or more) working years. Although they are not receiving as much publicity, men too face some confusing new options. Job changes and even second careers are much more acceptable now than in the past, and a man who has a working wife may have more freedom to make changes than he anticipated. Of course, these new options and pressures provide sources of imbalance and conflict in marriage, parenthood, and other types of relationships.

A job shift—whether it is small or major, whether it affects just ourselves or others close to us—will always be scary, even if it is exciting. The best thing that we can do for ourselves throughout our working lives is to try to be prepared emotionally, financially and vocationally to make change work *for* us when it comes our way.

Mid-life Shift (Ages 40 to 50)

The age 40 transition is the eye of the storm—the warm front of all the dreams pursued since childhood bumping into the cold front of reality. Limitations of time, ability, and opportunity collide. This can be a sad time for workers who have fallen short of a dream.

The big culprit in this rude awakening at the 40 year mark is the maturity myth that most of us bought into during our teens and 20's. If we did what we were supposed to do, instead of exploring our own inclinations, we are expecting a reward at this stage of life. If the promises have not come true, and we are not safe, secure, and stable, we feel cheated and outraged. If the promises have come true, our lives may be boring, repetitive, and unexciting, and we feel cheated and outraged. The maturity myth is a development catch-22: it gets us either way.

People who are unhappy with their personal or vocational lives at this time may again re-examine their values and beliefs. Those who feel that doing what they were supposed to do did not reward them may decide that there is something else they *want* to do. People who do not discover a happy ending in their present job may decide to take more risks. Many people leave jobs to start over, go back to school, become self-employed, or do something they have always wanted to do. Women whose changing attitudes and values have caused them to outgrow old roles may start school and/or work. For more and more people, a series of different vocations is beginning to make sense, because we grow and change, and because our productive and energetic years are being prolonged. It does not make sense to be stagnant in one job all your life or dead-ended in one at age 40. This is especially true since, in the current economy, the promised security is often not forthcoming anyway. Companies are bought and merged, jobs or whole departments are phased out by changes in policy or management, highly paid executives are let go to save money on salaries or to avoid paying retirement benefits.

More people are taking risks, retraining in their 30's, 40's, or 50's, changing jobs if the old one is a compromise, starting new businesses at 50 or second careers after retirement. When life expectancies were shorter, facing your disappointments and unfinished dreams at 40 might have been an invitation to depression; now it can be the beginning of a new reality, based upon the opportunity to be the new you. People who value highly something about their present job (for example, security, salary, or location), may not want to leave it. Instead, they may shift their search for personal fulfillment or recognition to hobbies, community involvement, or family activities. They may find new challenge and fulfillment in taking the role of mentor to a younger colleague. Reevaluation of jobs, roles or values by one or both partners in a relationship may create a need for change in the balance of the family. A former full-time housewife may begin exploring jobs, hobbies or further education, or she may want more company from her husband if the children are grown. A man at this age could be gearing up for a promotion, want to try a new career, or be ready to devote more time to family and leisure. A husband and wife whose activities and needs can be balanced at this stage may find they have more time than ever to spend relating to each other and developing leisure activities. For ourselves and significant others, these are tasks that developmental theorist Havighurst (1950) has identified as those that most Americans do not accomplish until middle age. The fact that these essential things remain undone until this age clearly spotlights the pressures the first two decades of adulthood put on us. The awareness of limitations and lost dreams that often comes at this stage can be painful. The important thing to remember vocationally is that at 40, we will still have at least 25 working years ahead. Although it is sometimes more difficult to get a job at 40 than 25, there are many ways and many enterprises where age and experience offer real advantages.

Refocusing (Ages 50 to 60)

If we are to live constructively and postively from age 50 on, we must possess integrity in many senses of the word. We need the kind

of integrity that stems from internal motivation, from self-determi-
nation and self-reward, because many of the life activities that generated external approval, such as work and child raising, are drawing
to a close. And we need the kind of integrity that comes from the
root of the word, integrate, to face and accept as a part of ourselves
the inevitable aging, lost dreams, and mistakes that we cannot undo.
For those who have dealt with these realities and determined to move
on, the 50's can indeed be a time of redirection. Even as we become
concerned about dwindling time and health, these same limitations
sharpen our sense of the preciousness of our remaining years. The
work society designated as ours is largely done, and there is an
unhurried feeling, a redefinition of values where other human beings
become more important and money and power less so.

Many people at this age develop new activities and goals to implement this new outlook on life. With ever-increasing affluence and
spectacular strides in health care, many in this age group are ex-
tending and enjoying their years prior to retirement. They may start
businesses, begin new full- and part-time work, give time to community action, or develop leisure pursuits such as hobbies and travel.
These ways of branching out are also great beginnings for a necessary
learning process, that of structuring one's own time, something many
people never have to do until retirement.

Redirection (Ages 65 and On)

To those of us wrapped up in college, jobs, or families, the idea
of waking up one morning with permission to do nothing sounds
like a dream. Retirement is something most of us look forward to
and store up postponed dreams for in our busiest years. However,
the approach or arrival of that moment causes anxiety or depression
in many people. Work, a source of social contacts, recognition, and
structure has been removed from our lives. In addition to income,
that paycheck provided reassurance that we were needed and appreciated. Replacing these activities and learning to provide those
feelings for oneself takes time and often help and support.

An additional problem of retirement is the psychological impact of
the concept itself. There is prejudice against older people. We often
picture them in cartoons as incompetent drivers, jealously guarding
their fixed incomes and shaking their gray heads at the younger
generation. We isolate the elderly, in part because they remind us
that old age and death wait for each of us; consequently, our attitudes
cannot help but convey the idea that this is all we have to look
forward to. Many older people do have real reasons to worry about

dependence, ill health, financial problems, and loneliness. But for as many others, nothing but that fear itself is standing in the way of another 15 or 20 years of active enjoyment of life, and continued growth. They can try new activities and pursue long delayed leisure interests. They can feel satisfied with the contributions they have made, and can continue to share their wisdom, memories, perspectives, and knowledge in part-time jobs, volunteer capacities, or with younger friends and relatives.

The work of growth is seldom easy and never completed. The realization that maturity is a process and not a condition gives us hope; it gives us permission to be unfinished, to make mistakes, to ask for help. We can continually recreate ourselves and our lives. We can change our minds, alter our lifestyles, experiment with new ideas, acquire new skills, accept new challenges, and start over. New learning and new beginnings are always available. We can now be comfortable with the knowledge that we will never be finished growing.

---

1. From *The Nature of Human Values* (Free Press, 1973). Copyright by Milton Rokeach, 1967. Reproduced by permission of Halgren Tests, 873 Persimmon Ave., Sunnyvale, Calif. 94087.

EXPLORING YOUR PERSONAL VALUES

We have already seen that our values, attitudes and beliefs govern our decisions and behaviors, both small and large. Our values reflect what is most important to each of us. An incomplete awareness of our values can interfere with effective decision making, lead us to make conflicting choices, or lead us to act in ways that we may later regret.

For these reasons, examining our own values is one of the critical steps in the decision-making cycle; it is an essential basis for self-assessment and self-understanding. If our decisions are to lead us where we want to go, we must first have a clear idea of where that is.

Following is a list of thirteen values that the psychologist, Milton Rokeach, suggests we may exercise through our daily choices and activities.[1] To help you gain a clearer picture of your values and of how they have emerged and changed over time, and to help you determine if your current actions match your values, this activity requires that you rate each value on the three dimensions:

1. A value that I held when I was younger.
2. A value that I have held but am questioning now.
3. A value that I hold now.

Spaces are provided after each value listed for you to rate it on these three dimensions. Place a number (1 through 5) in each space to indicate how strongly you hold that value. A "5" would indicate a very important value, and a "1" a least important value. You need not mark any value that you have not held in the past and do not hold now. When you have finished all three columns, consider the relative importance of all 13 values in your life. Using the boxes on the right, rank each value by giving it a number from 1 (most important) to 13 (least important).

Personal Values

Achievement–Recognition–Status

Younger   Question   Now

Feeling satisfaction for a job well done or a challenge well met. Receiving approval or attention from those whose opinions you respect. Achieving status in line with your talents and achievements.

Aesthetic Considerations

Younger *Question* *Now*

Having the opportunities and time to appreciate the beauty in people, art, nature, your surroundings, or whatever else you consider lovely and important. ____ ____ ____ ☐

Challenging Opportunities

Having opportunities to use your creativity, your training, your intelligence, and your other talents. Facing a variety of challenges rather than the routine. Having the freedom to try new ideas or creative approaches. ____ ____ ____ ☐

Health—Physical and Mental

Feeling good in a physical sense. Being relatively free of anxieties, "hang-ups," and feelings of being harried that can hinder your peace of mind. ____ ____ ____ ☐

Income–Wealth

Significantly improving your financial position. Obtaining those things that money can buy. ____ ____ ____ ☐

Independence

Having the freedom to "do your own thing" either on or off the job. Having time flexibility. Having control over your own actions. ____ ____ ____ ☐

Love–Personal Relationships–Family

Caring for, sharing with, and giving to those who are close to you such as family and peers. Being generous, sympathetic, loyal, and helpful to those you love. Having the time to devote to personal relationships. ____ ____ ____ ☐

Morality

Maintaining without conflict your moral, ethical, and/or religious standards whatever their source. Being able to accept the goals, values, and standards of your organization.

Younger *Question* *Now*

_____ _____ _____ ☐

Pleasure–Fun

Having a good time. Enjoying the company of others. Having the time to play. Making new friends.

_____ _____ _____ ☐

Power

The ability to influence or control others. Getting others to follow the course of action you prefer.

_____ _____ _____ ☐

Security

Feeling safe. Feeling free of continual concern about the dangers of unexpected and/or unpleasant changes. Having the essentials you need.

_____ _____ _____ ☐

Self-Development

Increasing your wisdom, maturity, learning, and understanding of life for their own sake. Becoming a more rounded person. Having the time to pursue intellectual interests.

_____ _____ _____ ☐

Service to Others

Being a useful member of the groups with which you identify. Knowing you have accomplished things that will benefit others.

_____ _____ _____ ☐

To get the maximum benefit from this form of self-analysis try to use the information you have generated to answer the following questions for each value category:

1. Where did I first encounter this value? Have my feelings about it changed over time? If they have, what led to the change?
2. Is this a value I am questioning now? Why? What effect would giving it up or altering it have on my lifestyle?
3. If I hold this value now, do I frequently exercise it? How? If not, why not? What might I do to minimize any discrepancy?
4. Where does this value rank on my list? What does that tell me about myself? What does this value contribute to my picture of the ideal job?

The goal of this exercise has been to gain a better understanding of your values, which will help you choose vocational goals that reflect the ideal you. They will help you decide how you wish to spend your time and what rewards you desire. Such self-awareness will also help you maintain a stable sense of who you are during the personal and professional changes and events that will come with the various life stages just discussed.

As we go on to examine other aspects of the career-decision process, your values will combine with your skills, interests, aptitudes and experiences to help you identify a preferred lifestyle, the type and level of job that suits you, and the kinds of enterprises you might wish to work in. Later, these elements of self-awareness will affect how you implement your job campaign and do your job.

DECISIONS AND VALUES

You have already explored both the decision-making process and your own values. In the following exercise several vignettes provide a chance for you to examine decision making and values in action.[1] After reading the description of each situation, think about what values are involved, what alternatives the people in the situation might have, what course of action you would choose in that particular case, and what your reasoning was.

Jim has to declare a major soon, and he can't decide what to do. He has always wanted to be a doctor like his dad, and has taken mostly pre-med courses. Jim's counselor says that he is really not sure whether Jim will be able to get into medical school. His grades have been good, but not spectacular. The way Jim sees it, he can take two more years of pre-med and risk "wasting" that time or he can decide right now to switch to a related major, such as something in the field of biochemistry or an allied medical profession.

1. What values can you identify as being involved here?

achievement / family

_____

_____

2. What alternatives do you see for Jim?

_____

_____

_____

3. What course of action do you think would be best for him?

_____

_____

1. Adapted from an exercise created by Cinda Field Wells, Ph.D., Dale Alexander, A.C.S.W. and Pat Jonas, M.D., The Ohio State University, March, 1980.

4. Which of your own values are you displaying in suggesting this course of action?

_____

_____

_____

   Peggy is in business school. Her father has a big accounting firm and has always planned on having Peggy become his partner after college since she is the best mathematician in the family. Peggy likes accounting, but since starting college she has been longing to explore some of the other careers she has heard about, especially teaching. Her friends envy her because she has a secure, high-paying job waiting for her in accounting. They tell her she'd be crazy to change to education. Her father would be terribly disappointed, and she'd be out there, along with a lot of other teachers, competing for a limited number of jobs.

1. What values can you identify as being involved?

_____

_____

_____

2. What alternatives do you see for Peggy?

_____

_____

_____

3. What course of action do you think would be best for her?

_____

_____

4. Which of your own values are you displaying in suggesting this course of action?

_____

_____

_____

Jerry likes people and has always been good at handling their personalities and problems. He feels he'd be successful in a business setting, such as sales or public relations. He also likes the idea of helping people, and has been interested in counseling the handicapped, which he did one summer as a volunteer. Even though he's not sure he'd like working with some of the business executives he knows, he's leaning toward business. He thinks the business world would probably be more exciting, and he is sure it will be more financially rewarding than counseling. He likes children and wants to be able to support a large family and to afford a big house, vacations, and maybe a boat.

1. What values can you identify as being involved?

_____

_____

_____

2. What alternatives do you see for Jerry?

_____

_____

_____

3. What course of action do you think would be best for him?

_____

_____

_____

4. Which of your own values are you displaying in suggesting this course of action?

_____

_____

_____

Marianne is 31 and has been back in school a few months. She quit college in her senior year when she and her husband had their first baby. Their children are 10 and 7 now, and Marianne wants to finish school and get a job working with computers. Tonight, though, she's asking herself if it's worth it. She has two tests coming up, she wants to clean the house for company, and one of the children is sick. Her husband isn't crazy about the idea of her working, and she's beginning to wonder if he's right.

1. What values can you identify as being involved?

_____

_____

_____

2. What alternatives do you see for Marianne?

_____

_____

_____

3. What course of action do you think would be best for her?

_____

---

4. Which of your own values are you displaying in suggesting this course of action?

REFERENCES

Gould, R. "The Phases of Adult Life: A Study in Developmental Psychology," *American Journal of Psychiatry*, 1972.

Havighurst, R. J. *Developmental Tasks and Education*, New York: Longmans Green, 1950.

Levision, O. *The Psychological Development of Men in Early Adulthood and the Mid-Life Transition*, Minneapolis: University of Minnesota Press, 1974.

O'Neill, N. and O'Neill, G. *Shifting Gears*, New York: M. Evans and Company, 1974.

Sheehy, G. *Passages: Predictable Crises of Adult Life*, New York: E. P. Dutton and Co., Inc., 1976.

Super, D. E., et al. *Vocational Development: A Framework for Research*, New York: Teachers College, Columbus University Bureau of Publications, 1957.

Yankelovich, Daniel. "The New Psychological Contracts at Work," *Psychology Today*, May 1978, pp. 46–50.

5

Paths in the Workplace

When Alice, wandering in Wonderland, asked the Cheshire cat how to get out of the woods, he replied, "That depends upon where you want to go."

Lewis Carroll

Like Alice, each of us will have to make a number of different choices as we pursue our careers. Decisions about which field to enter, moving up the ladder, or moving out, are all choices we must make once or more during our lives. People we meet along the way may try to help us with these decisions, but the choices of when we start, where we go, and the turns we take are still ours. Thus, our careers—the different occupational directions we take throughout our lives—are really personal paths we create for ourselves as we travel our individual ways.

The *career paths* we follow greatly affect our views of ourselves. What we do for a living gives us a personal reference point in society and may strongly influence our lifestyles. It influences how we live, where we live, and the relationships we form. The everyday process of getting acquainted reflects this special status of work in our society. When people first meet, their conversations often start with references to work: "What's your job (or major)?" "What do you plan to do when you graduate?" When asked, "Who are you?" most people respond, "a teacher," "a student," or "a homemaker" rather than "an extrovert" or "a U. S. citizen."

The importance of work in determining how members of our society view themselves was demonstrated in a survey conducted by the Target Group Index, a national adult survey. Published in *Working Women* in March 1979, this survey of some 30,000 people—8,300 of whom were women—found that women who were working described themselves in more positive terms than nonworking women. Generally speaking, working women tended to rate themselves higher than nonworking women in terms of their ability to get along with and support others, their self-assurance, intellect, and humor. Given that so much emphasis is placed on the importance of work by members of our society, it is not surprising that being uncertain or undecided about a college major or occupation may make us feel guilty or embarassed.

While research indicates that the majority of students will change majors at least once during college, and will do the same in work after they graduate, many students still believe that there is one right occupation for them. Their choices may thus appear to be scary and irreversible. Perhaps this is what Robert Frost meant when he described his decision to become a poet:

The Road Not Taken[1]

Two roads diverged in a yellow wood,
And sorry I could not travel both
And be one traveler, long I stood
And looked down one as far as I could
To where it bent in the undergrowth.

Then took the other, as just as fair,
And having perhaps the better claim,
Because it was grassy and wanted wear;
Though as for that the passing there
Had worn them really about the same.

And both that morning equally lay
In leaves no step had trodden black.
Oh, I kept the first for another day!
Yet knowing how way leads on to way,
I doubted if I should ever come back.

I shall be telling this with a sigh
Somewhere ages and ages hence:
Two roads diverged in a wood, and I—
I took the one less traveled by,
And that has made all the difference.

Robert Frost

It may be true that some individuals will follow only one path, but for most of us our careers will reflect a number of paths and choices. Because of this, it is likely that we will be able to clearly see the paths we have followed only in the latter parts of our lives. Regardless of the number of pathways we each take, all of our careers will share the common element of personal choices and development. One of the things we need most to start along this journey is a view of the possibilities that are open to us.

1. From *The Poetry of Robert Frost*. Edited by Edward Connery Lathem. Copyright 1916, © 1969 by Holt, Rinehart and Winston. Copyright 1944 by Robert Frost. Reprinted by permission of Holt, Rinehart and Winston, Publishers.

WHERE AM I GOING?
A MAP OF THE WORLD OF WORK

The Canadian educator, Gerald Cosgrave (1973), has provided us with a useful tool for exploring the world of work. He suggested that the workplace can be broken down into three dimensions: types of work, levels of work, and kinds of work. These three categories can be arranged to form a cube, a three-dimensional map that organizes occupations according to their commonalities. Figure 5.1 illustrates this for us.

Types of Work

Earlier we explored how John Holland's worker personality types can be used to explain why people gravitate toward particular activities. As is shown on the face of Figure 5.1, Cosgrave believes that Holland's system can also be used to describe work settings and occupations. Like Holland, Cosgrave believes that people *create their work environments.* Although a particular work setting is organized around common tasks, it is more than that. It is a social fabric woven around common tastes, problems, interests, and ideals. The unifying element in each environment is its personality type. Figure 5.2 illustrates how particular types are more likely to cluster in certain occupations. The same guidelines that were used to describe personality types apply to the occupational types in Figure 5.2. That is, persons who work in occupations that are adjacent to each other share more in common than they do with people working in occupations that are across the hexagon.

When it is flexibly used, Holland's system can be a useful tool for describing people in different work situations. Although a particular occupation may be characterized as a particular type, the people it describes are not as easily stereotyped. Different jobs within occupations have different rewards and demands. Accounting, for example, is shown on the hexagon as primarily a conventional (C) work setting. However, it may also have enterprising (E), social (S), and investigative (I) elements. A person with a CES personality pattern who likes enterprising and social activities may seek out and perform the persuasive and supervisory aspects of an accounting job. The person with the CIE personality pattern might enjoy analytical and theoretical tasks. Both individuals may be very successful accountants, but in different positions. If the CES accountant is asked to perform more investigative tasks, he or she might become dissatisfied with the job. To resolve this situation, the accountant would be faced

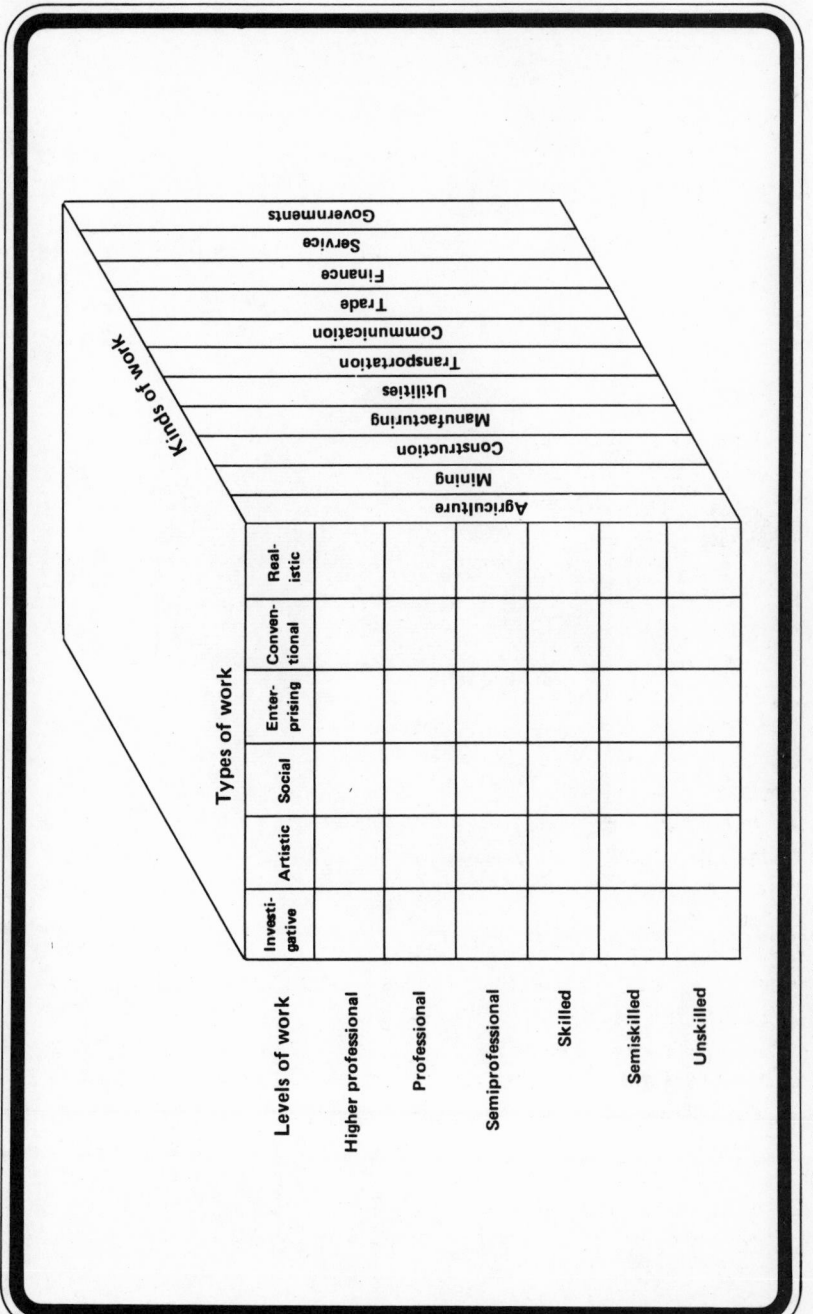

Figure 5.1 The World of Work Cube. (From Gerald Cosgrave, Career Planning: Search for a Future. Prepared by Dorothy Mould. Reproduced by permission of the Guidance Centre, © 1973 by the Governing Council of the University of Toronto. Reprinted by permission.)

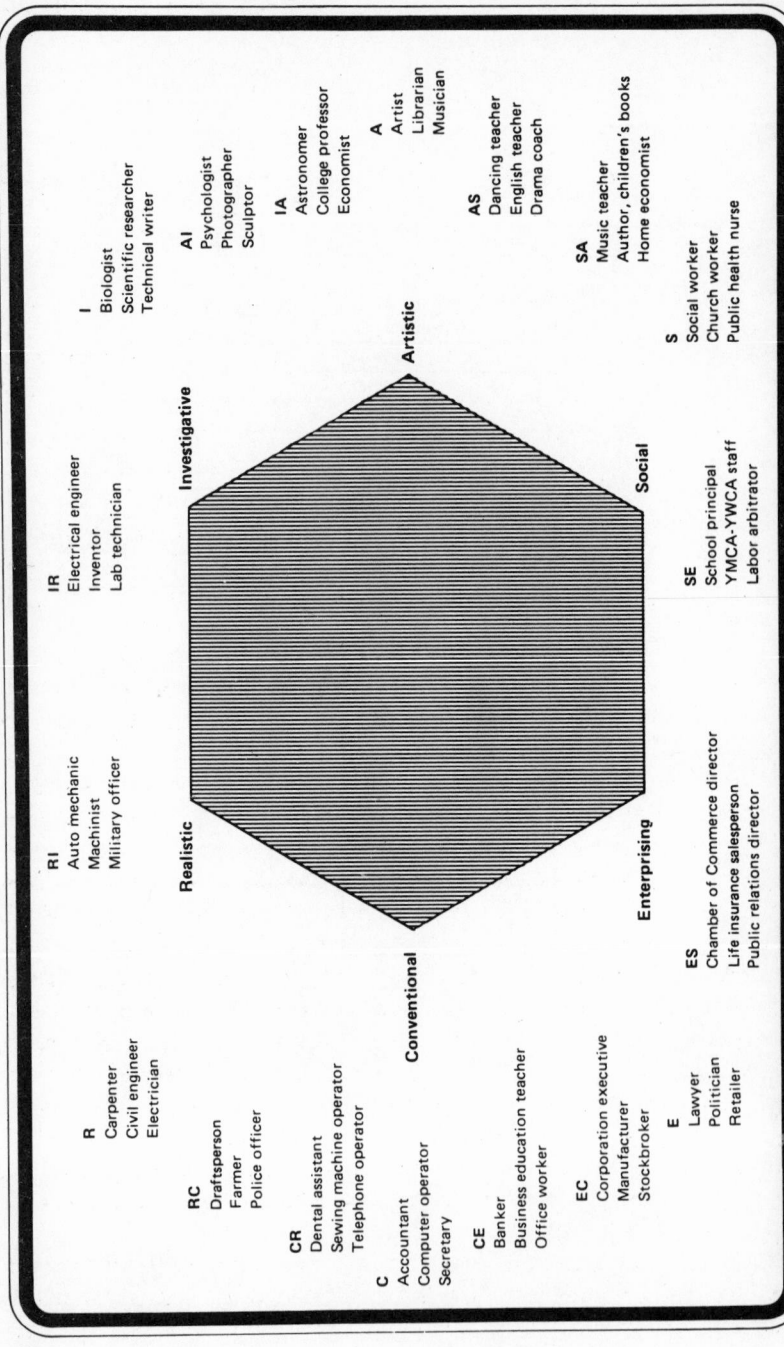

Figure 5.2 Work Environments. (From D. Campbell, *If You Don't Know Where You're Going, You'll End Up Somewhere Else.* Niles, Illinois, Argus

with the choice of changing his or her preferences, renegotiating responsibilities, or changing to another position that agrees more with his or her personality.

Levels of Work

Several decades ago in Cincinnati, 1658 students in public schools were asked to state their occupational choices. The results of this survey were summarized by Dale (1948, p. 419) in these words:

> "What would Cincinnati be like if these students became sole inhabitants of the city in the jobs of their choices, ten years from now? . . . Health services would be very high, with every eighteen people supporting one doctor. . . . It may be, however, that they would all be needed in a city that had no garbage disposal workers, no laundry workers, and no water supply since no one chose to do that kind of work. . . . The two bus drivers . . . will find that their customers get tired of waiting, and use the services of the sixty-seven airline pilots. It may be difficult getting to Crosley Field to see the forty baseball players.

There have been many other studies of the occupational plans and expectations of students. Like Dale's study, all of them point to the widespread belief that everyone should strive for the highest rung of the occupational ladder.

Our society needs people working in all fields and at all levels to make it go. Cosgrave suggested that there are six general levels in our society. People at the higher levels have more responsibility for making decisions and supervising others than those working at the lowest levels. Starting at the lowest rung on the ladder, the six levels on Cosgrave's cube are: (1) *unskilled work* is simple and routine and requires little independent decision making or creativity; (2) *semiskilled jobs* demand some minimal skill and knowledge or a high degree of manipulative skill in a limited range of tasks; (3) *skilled occupations* require expert skills, specialized knowledge and judgment in carrying out assigned duties; (4) *semiprofessional and managerial jobs* involve mental tasks demanding specialized knowledge or judgment; (5) *professional jobs* require considerable knowledge and judgment; and (6) *higher professional and managerial jobs* require a high level of knowledge, mental ability and autonomy.

Levels 5 and 6 require college or even graduate school training. Levels 3 and 4 demand high school, college, or other specialized training. Levels 1 and 2 require on-the-job training, or perhaps none at all.

In Figure 5.3 we see how the skills that are required in a particular work environment may be built upon through different levels of education and training to achieve different occupational objectives.

The medical professions offer an example of how a common set of investigative skills may be refined by attending two-year or four-year programs to enter different levels of work within the same professional area. Many people are interested in medicine, but they differ in their interests, abilities, personality, finances, and the amount of authority and responsibility they want to assume at work. Those who aspire to and have the capacity for high levels of achievement might attend a professional college, and wind up as surgeons, doctors, medical researchers, or head nurses. Other students might attend two-year programs to be trained as medical technologists, physician's assistants, paramedics, or practical nurses. Persons who do not elect to get training beyond high school might find on-the-job training opportunities and become aids or orderlies.

The skill levels are shown in Figures 5.1 and 5.3. A person trained in a medically related specialty at the two-year level may decide to advance in his or her career by seeking a four-year college degree in a related area and perhaps later attaining a graduate or professional medical specialty degree. Similarly a commercial artist who has artistic skills may be moving up the ladder from the two-year technical training he or she received to a higher professional level by pursuing an advanced degree. We may also find that the shop foreman may take night courses and move toward a managerial position that was vacated when the manager moved up as company president.

It is also important to note from Figure 5.3 how the same basic skills can be used across a variety of occupations and settings. This is particularly helpful to keep in mind when it comes to job hunting after graduation. For example, teachers facing a tight job market may use their instructional skills in business as salespersons, staff development specialists, public relations specialists, and managerial trainees.

All of this suggests that once you have an idea of the fields or types of work that appeal to you, you need to further explore your values, abilities and desires to decide at what level in your field you want to start, and what level you might ultimately want to reach. It also suggests that in exploring the world of work you should be aware of how the same set of skills can be transferred to different work settings.

Cosgrave notes that although each person in our society is free to aim as high as his or her potential permits, striving to reach the top may not be as important as it sometimes seems. And it can also be unwise. Being at too high a level puts constant pressure on a worker. Too much pressure may cause considerable strain and physical, emotional, and interpersonal damage. Reaching for ever higher levels of achievement in order to please or keep up with others may thus become a trap if the work does not also provide personal pleasure and satisfaction.

To avoid the possibility of reaching too high too soon, Cosgrave suggests that you may wish to start by defining the level where you will be most comfortable and setting a series of moderate goals for yourself. The goals then act like a series of steps where you move on to the next after mastering the prior one. If you use this procedure, you will find that your distant goal is more tentative and less over-whelming, and you will have room for further investigation and redecision.

Beginning at a moderate level does not mean you must stay there, or that your talent is being wasted. One advantage is that such a job gives you a chance to learn the ropes and make mistakes in a situation where you are not ultimately responsible. The "whiz kid" who steps into a higher job in full view of the company brass is under a lot more pressure not to learn by trial and error.

No matter where you start, nor how high you aim in the world of work, a time will probably come when you reach your ceiling. If upward movement continues, it may bring you to a level of respon-sibility which is beyond your competence or which you feel demands too much time and energy. Laurence Peter (1967) believes that this happens frequently and is a prime cause of inefficiency in our society. His "Peter Principle" states that, "In time, every post tends to be occupied by an employee who is incompetent to carry out his/her duties." The remedy is to halt advancement just below this level.

It may be difficult to realize that you have reached a ceiling when your present work is performed well. You may go through a period of anxiety and uncertainty at this time in your career; the rewards of moving up in the hierarchy may look as though they outweigh the problems, a trap of rising expectations. Other ways of dealing with the challenge might be a move to another position at the same level within your organization or to try to expand the duties and respon-sibilities within your present position.

Places of Work

The third dimension Cosgrave has identified includes 11 broad occupational clusters, each comprising a certain type of enterprise. Although you may prefer certain enterprises because of their pur-poses, surroundings or personnel, it is important to remember that

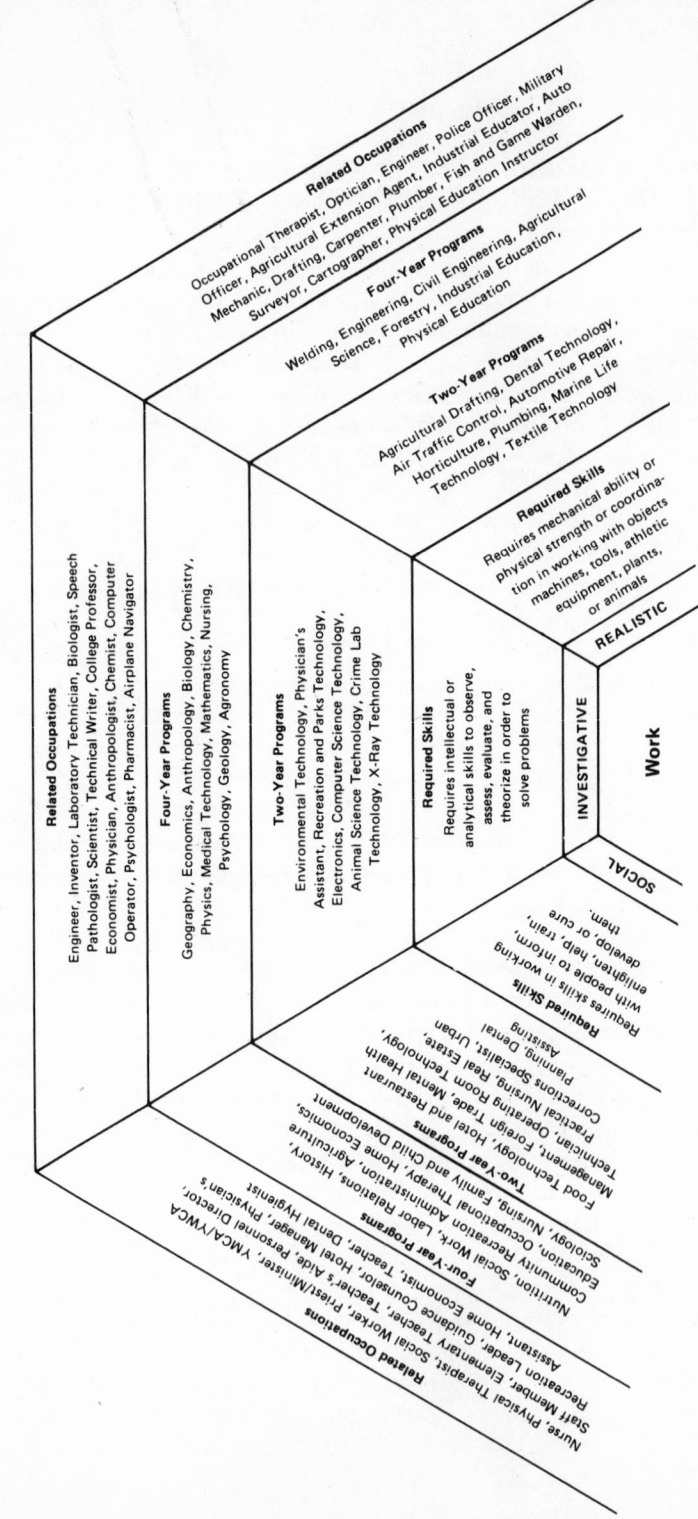

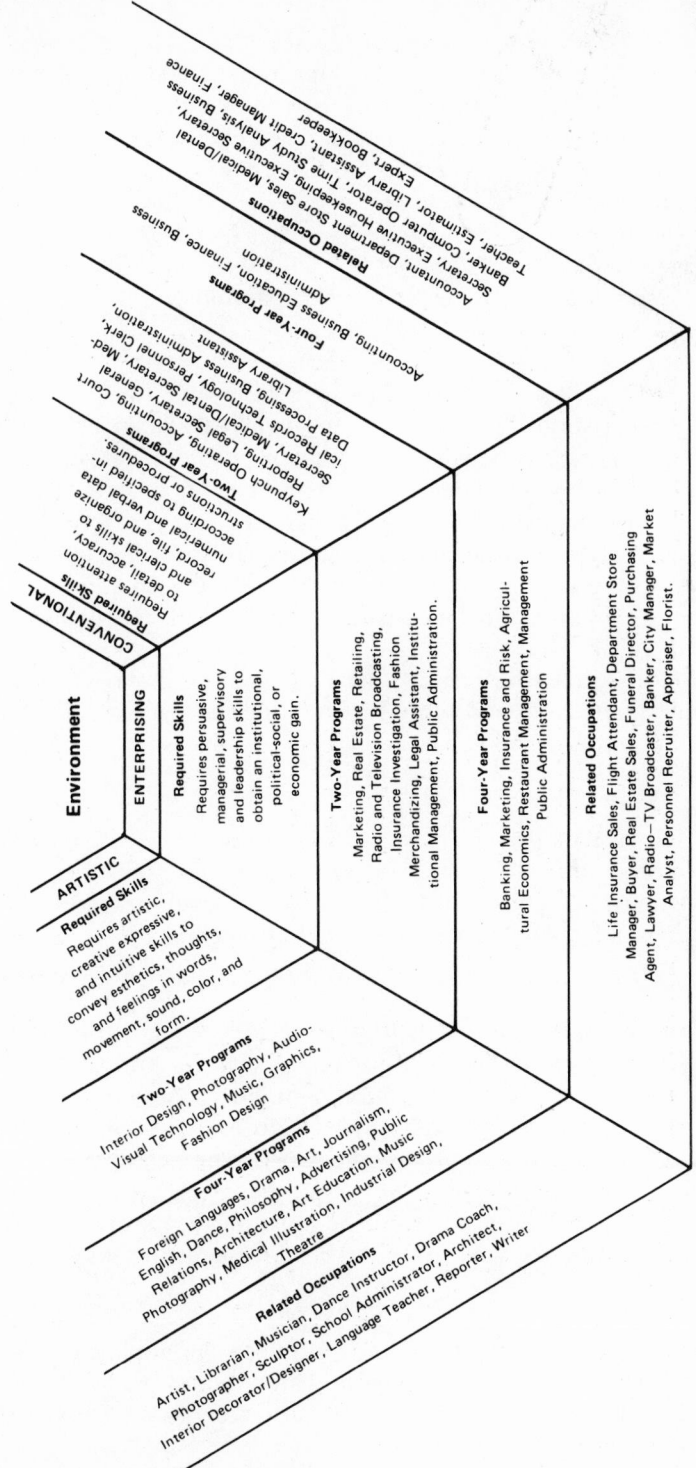

Figure 5.3 Levels of education and related occupations.

the same types and levels of work can be performed across a variety of enterprises. Clerical, teaching, or numerical skills are needed in many occupational settings other than the most obvious ones. Keeping this in mind will help you see a broader range of opportunities for yourself in today's tight job market.

As you read through the kinds of enterprises listed below, try to identify several areas that appeal to you and what you like about them. Try to imagine how some of your skills and interests could be used in each area.

Agriculture.   Agriculture, which takes in fishing and forestry, includes many occupations that would fit the label "realistic." Unskilled work in this area might involve physical labor or maintenance on a farm, a park, or a resort. Other such jobs require more education, such as breeding dairy cattle, managing a fish hatchery, or reforesting a lumber site. Professional-level jobs could range from heading an oceanography expedition to managing the parks and recreation program of a large city, or running a landscaping or agricultural business.

Mining.   Mining industries need unskilled labor, trained workers such as mine inspectors, and more highly educated people such as geologists, mining engineers, and researchers on extraction and use of minerals.

Construction.   The construction industry requires unskilled laborers as well as numerous skilled tradespeople—carpenters, electricians, masons, welders and other realistic types. Higher level professionals whose work is related to construction include architects and engineers, who may be investigative and conventional as well as realistic.

Manufacturing.   Manufacturing is a vast network of industries that includes jobs in almost any area of interest. Common jobs at levels 1 and 2 are assembly line worker and foreman. Level 3 and 4 workers might be managers or technicians who design and run equipment and plants. The upper levels in these enterprises can include product testers, researchers or engineers. Although many of these jobs are realistic or investigative, social people are also needed in personnel and public relations, as well as enterprising talents in sales and advertising.

Utilities.   Our utilities require a large number of employees for function and upkeep. Lower levels in this area require realistic and conventional interests. Examples are repair persons, switchboard operators and clerks. Level 3 and 4 jobs may include managing levels 1 and 2, or may be more social or enterprising, such as sales managers and public relations specialists. People with the highest level of education in these industries might be the engineers, who solve problems and develop new products, or top level managers with financial specialties.

Transportation. Transport includes many semiskilled jobs such as loading, delivery, dispatcher, trucker, or airline steward. The next level includes jobs such as fleet management, vehicle repair, or highway inspection. Highest levels of training would include airline pilot, urban planner, or highway designer.

Communication. Communication fields expand to include almost all of Holland's six categories, although there are fewer semiskilled jobs here than in many areas. One example might be an apprentice technician with radio or TV equipment. Many entry level jobs require an intermediate level of skill or education, such as newspaper reporter, copy editor for a publisher, or a TV camera operator or photographer. Professional level jobs may require substantial experience and/or skill. These might include news manager for a TV station, newspaper editor, publicity, or public relations and advertising executives, or more glamorous jobs such as TV commentator, foreign correspondent, or novelist.

Trade. Trade and related enterprises offer many areas where a relatively untrained worker can start. Some are realistic, such as loading trucks, or stocking retail stores. Others require conventional interests, such as inventory ordering or cashiering. Still others require social and enterprising persons such as sales people or produce demonstrators. Jobs with more training or experience include buyer, department manager, or regional sales representative. Advertising employs people with artistic interests for copy writing, photography or layout and design. The highest level jobs often involve enterprising and social skills for managing employees or buying for whole areas or chains. Also employed at this level may be personnel or labor relations experts, industrial and consulting psychologists, educators, and public relations people. Many large companies have programs that permit an entry-level worker to work up to or train for middle or higher level jobs with the firm.

Finance. Finance often attracts people with conventional and enterprising characteristics. One may begin in this area as a bank teller, or clerk for an insurance or loan company. Jobs with more responsibilities are auditor or loan officer. Higher-level jobs might be as an accountant or financial manager for a business.

Service. The service industries include jobs where something is being done for someone, and for this reason attract many social and enterprising types. Persons at levels 1 and 2 could be a hospital orderly, a hotel or restaurant employee, or a volunteer in a helping profession. Jobs in service areas requiring some training include beautician or barber, lab technician or probation officer. Higher-level professionals include doctors and nurses, psychologists, teachers, and museum curators.

Governments. City, county, and federal governments hire people for varied kinds of work at all levels. Many jobs available in private industries can be also done for the government. Admission and advancement in most government jobs is regulated by civil service tests which must be passed to qualify for a certain job or level. Exams for beginning-level jobs test literacy and common sense as well as specific skills. Such jobs include clerk–typist or mail carrier. Middle-level jobs include office management, law enforcement, and the inspection of government supported institutions such as schools and hospitals. High-level jobs include such varied positions as judge, environmental specialist or economist. Many government jobs—from dog catcher to U.S. President—are not under the civil service and are elected or appointed. These may require credentials or assets beyond one's ability or training, such as money for campaigns, political influence, and a willingness to take risks.

Your comfort, satisfaction and competence with a job rests on the interaction of the three elements we have discussed: type, level, and kind of job. You will need to investigate and evaluate the characteristics of your personality and skills and various work environments. Which combination of realistic, investigative, artistic, social, enterprising, and conventional qualities best describes you? Look at the levels—higher professional to unskilled—that lie within each of those types and within your areas of interests. Pinpoint the various enterprises and areas of interest that appeal to you and investigate the kinds of jobs they offer. Begin to evaluate how these match up with your aspirations and abilities. Job satisfaction is determined not by any single factor, but by the relationship among what we aspire to do, what we can do, and the rewards and demands at a specific level of work.

VALUES ANALYSIS

Eventually you will narrow your alernatives to the point where you can begin comparing specific careers or different options within one broad career area, such as law, medicine, computer science, or engineering. At this point the values we have dealt with so far may seem too general for making fine discriminations. The following exercise, therefore, is designed to help you learn how to break general value areas into more specific components that apply to specific job activities and requirements. It may help you to refer to other exercises and chapters in the book where some of these things are discussed. Stimulus questions have been provided for each value. See what additional questions you can generate on issues that are important to you, based both on what you have already learned about yourself and on feedback from group members, classmates, family, or friends. Additional value and questions that are important to you may be added at the end of the activity.

1. Achievement/Recognition/Status
   a. What achievement or kinds of achievements will make me most proud?
   b. By whom do I want to be recognized?

_____

_____

_____

_____

_____

2. Challenge/Pitting self against adversity
   a. What does challenge mean to me? Does it involve thinking, creating, problem solving, dealing with people, working with my hands, organizing?
   b. How will I know when something ceases to be challenging?

_____

_____

_____

_____

_____

3. Health—physical and mental
   a. What are my physical limitations, such as height, weight, energy, eyesight, strength?
   b. What are my mental and emotional limitations, such as intelligence, rate of thinking, memory, tolerance for stress, tolerance for conflict?

_____

_____

_____

_____

4. Income/Material goods/Financial security
   a. What kind of life-style do I want to lead? Roughly what income level will it require?
   b. What and how much (for example, time, energy) am I willing to give up to earn money?

_____

_____

_____

_____

5. Independence/Autonomy
   a. Do I want to have someone to tell me what to do, or do I want to figure it out for myself?
   b. Do I want to run my own business?

_____

_____

---

6. Love/Friendships/Family/Others
   a. Do I want to work with people?
   b. Would I like to be in a position of authority over others or work along with them?

---

7. Morality/Ethics
   a. How do I feel about the ethics and/or politics practiced in the profession I am considering?
   b. Would I want to work for the government or for private industry?

---

8. Pleasure/Fun/Leisure/Free time
   a. How much free time do I need in a day or week?
   b. How much time per week do I want to spend working? Do I want to work evenings, weekends, or holidays?

_____

_____

_____

9. Power/Influence
   a. Is it important to me to influence or control those around
      me?
   b. Do I enjoy being in charge and taking responsibility?

_____

_____

_____

_____

10. Security—financial or emotional
    a. Do I feel upset when things are ambiguous or change fre-
       quently?
    b. Am I bored when things do not change often?

_____

_____

_____

_____

11. Self-development/Growth
    a. What do I want to learn about myself while working?
    b. How far do I want to advance in terms of rank and pay?

_____

_____

_____

_____

_____

12. Service to others
    a. In what way do I want to help people?
    b. What kinds of people do I want to work with?

_____

_____

_____

_____

_____

13.

_____

_____

_____

_____

14.

_____

_____

_____

_____

15.

REFERENCES

Campbell, D. *If you don't know where you're going, you'll end up somewhere else.* Niles, Illinois: Argus Communications, 1974.

Cosgrave, G. P. *Career Planning: Search for A Future.* Toronto, Canada: University of Toronto Press, 1973.

Dale, R. V. N. To Youth Who Choose Blindly. *Occupations*, 1948, p. 419.

Holland, J. L. *Making Vocational Choices: A Theory of Careers.* Englewood Cliffs, N.J.: Prentice-Hall, 1973.

Latham, E. C. (Ed.) *The Poetry of Robert Frost.* New York: Holt, Rinehart, and Winston, 1944.

Peter, L. J. and **Hull, R.** *The Peter Principle.* New York: William Morrow and Company, 1967.

chapter 6

It All Has To Do With Life Needs And Styles

Living is—

Living is
  a thing you do
Now or never—
  which do you do?

Piet Hein

In the last chapter we saw how different occupations can be organized on a cube according to the type and level of work performed, and the kind of enterprise they are associated with. This chapter explores how the work that we do affects our life needs and styles; it also identifies ways of gathering and evaluating occupational information so that you can make occupational choices that fulfill your life goals.

It should be clear from previous chapters that the choice of a career involves more than simply selecting a college major or an occupation and pursuing that goal. As it provides us with resources for living, work fills our time, challenges our abilities, supports our leisure pursuits, and offers us a place to get recognition and an opportunity to form relationships with others. Because the work that we do has such a major effect on us, it is important that we understand how our work pursuits fulfill our needs and fit into the total pattern of our lives.

OUR BASIC LIFE NEEDS

According to Abraham Maslow, work helps us meet a number of important needs. His theory of human motivation assumes that human needs are arranged along a heirarchy. When the needs at one level of the heirarchy are satisfied, the next set of needs begins to seem more important and to press for satisfaction. At the base of the heirarchy lie our most primitive needs—hunger and thirst. While these physiological needs are relatively simple and self-centered, they are also the most potent for they support life itself. The second level on the heirarchy is associated with our need for safety. After we feel assured of three meals a day, we work to secure warmth and comfort, protection from harm, and a stable future. The third set of needs, which become our greatest concern after we have established the necessary security, is that of "belongingness" and love. Working with others provides us with opportunities for friendships, validation, identification with a group, and a sense of mutual purpose. We need to know that our identities, beliefs and problems are shared and validated by special groups within our culture. Besides work colleagues, such groups might include our neighbors, church, a women's group, fraternity brothers, young Democrats, or Weight Watchers. Esteem emerges as the fourth level of need on the heirarchy. Through work efforts and other personal commitments, we strive for a sense of competence, worth, and prestige. The fifth level of need, that of self-actualization, is more complex. It involves using work to realize our creativity and values to experience a sense of personal meaning and integrity. Our work and other life activities allow us the chance to know and understand the world around us, and to share wisdom and feel a part of something greater than ourselves.

Maslow's research suggests that we are likely to meet the needs at the upper stages of the need heirarchy only after we have sifted through and successfully coped with the basic needs that seem more pressing during our youth and early adulthood. He also suggests that the way we feel depends upon the degree to which our needs are satisfied. When our basic physiological and safety needs go unmet, we are apt to experience anger. When the needs that are higher on the heirarchy go unmet we are more likely to experience anxiety.

It is relatively easy to see how this heirarchy of needs operates in our daily lives. When I am really hungry, I am not apt to be thinking about the origin of life. If we take this example one step further, we can also see how our needs are tied closely to our values. If I have been hungry for a long time, I must make a decision about how I will obtain food. If I have the money, I can purchase it. If I am broke, I can borrow from others, or I can beg or steal it. If I value industriousness and honesty, I will look for a job to earn money for food. If these values aren't important to me, I might beg or steal from others to feed myself. What we do for a living is thus intimately bound to our views of why we live and how we live.

A LIFE-STYLE THEME

Because of popular advertising most of us have some acquaintance with the term "life-style." We frequently hear, for example, about the California life-style, the singles life-style, the executive life-style, and the life-style of the retirement community. These life-styles may differ from our own; because they are so different, each may have a special appeal to us. The snowbound midwesterner may envy the free and sunny life-style of the southern Californian. The bored toll-booth operator may enjoy the fantasy of becoming a jet-hopping young executive. Our daily lives thus reflect our attempts to reconcile the difference between what our fantasies and aspirations would have us do with the realities of what we are capable of achieving.

If you were asked to describe your own life-style, how would you do it? Two sociologists, P.J. Miller and G. Stoberg, suggest that you would most likely describe it in terms of how you spend your time. When we are not sleeping, most of us spend our time at our studies or work, engaging in leisure and recreation activities, or interacting with family and friends. Taken together, these three activities form a triangle that can be used to represent the pattern of our life-styles. This triangle is shown in Figure 6.1.

The life-style triangle can be viewed as a kind of ecosystem where we give and receive energy from our daily activities. During a typical day, we engage in some activities that deplete our energies and tire us out and others that restore our energies and refresh us. Energy giving and energy receiving are often related to a common goal. For example, we may work hard to earn money to support a leisure activity that we enjoy.

The degree to which we emphasize the different activities on the triangle varies at different times in our lives as well as from day to day. The young child has little interest in the work of the adult and spends time and energy playing and interacting with the family. On the other hand, the college student who has spent several day cramming for exams knows what it's like to be exhausted by too much work, and dreams of free time to spend at leisure and recreational pursuits, or with supportive family and friends.

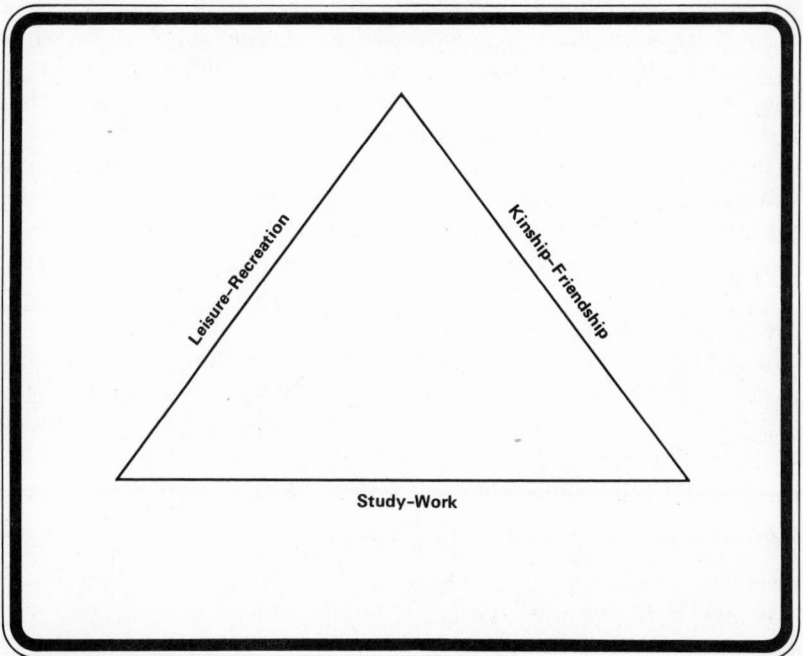

Figure 6.1   *The Life-style Triangle. (From Miller and Sjoberg, "Urban Middle-Class Life-styles in Transition." Journal of Applied Behavioral Sciences, 1973. Reprinted by permission.)*

The way we balance the activities on the life-style triangle has a great deal to do with how we view our lives. Too much or too little of any of the activities on the triangle can make our lives a joy or a struggle. Brief periods of imbalance in our activities will occur throughout our lives and we can manage them by finding an appropriate balance; in fact, periods of imbalance serve to challenge us and keep us in touch with ourselves. Research on human motivation shows that when things have been in harmony for too long, people become bored and seek to upset the balance of things as a way of creating new challenges for themselves.

How comfortable we are with our work is in part determined by how effective we are at matching our energy levels with the requirements of our jobs. Herman Wells, former President of Indiana University, vividly described his balancing act as a top-level executive when he jokingly said that a university president should be born with "the physical stamina of a Greek athlete, the cunning of Machiavelli, the wisdom of Solomon, the courage of a lion, and above all, the stomach of a goat." According to a 1975 survey by *Change* magazine, university presidents such as Dr. Wells spend as much as 100 hours per week at their jobs. Like doctors and many executives, their periods of rest are in constant jeopardy due to unanticipated crises. And, unless they have a great deal of stamina or can get away frequently, they may be too tired or "burnt out" to enjoy time spent with their families or at leisure and recreational pursuits.

In recent years, a growing number of corporations have become sensitive to the executive "burn-out syndrome" that occurs when a person takes on responsibilities that extend beyond the limits of his or her available energies. This syndrome is a frequent cause of job dissatisfaction, decreased efficiency, and strained relationships. Interestingly, it is not uncommon for people who have been working under pressure for long periods of time to develop minor illnesses such as colds when the pace of the job abruptly slows down. If a person works too long without a restful break more severe ailments may develop such as chronic fatigue, sleeplessness, high blood pressure, ulcers, and depression.

All of this suggests that in order for you to feel satisfied with your career, you will need to plan a life-style that balances your time, energies, capabilities, and needs with the demands and rewards of your work. Depending upon how highly you value work, you have at least two life-style options. Many Americans, especially those concerned with upward social mobility, view work as the benchmark of their lives and support it by their nonwork activities. Others see work as a means of providing the necessities of life, and its value is gauged in relation to how well it supports their nonwork pursuits. Which life-style do you prefer?

THE PYRAMID OF LIFE

Colin Turnbull's (1973) study of the Ik tribe of Uganda offers a vivid example of how people alter their life-style when their basic needs go unfulfilled. With the division of Africa into states, the Ik were excluded from many countries and were forced to discontinue their nomadic life-style. They lost contact with other tribes of the region, with whom they had traded their handmade weapons and mountain grown tobacco for dairy products and other goods.

Survival needs forced the Ik to experiment with new life-styles. Hunting and gathering in the barren mountain area to which they were confined proved totally inadequate. Terrace farming proved a failure because of scant rainfall and a four-year drought cycle. They next tried to sell their intimate knowledge of the mountains by acting as guides, spies, and intermediaries in the business of cattle raiding. They quickly learned to play one tribe off against another, selling their services to the highest bidder and blacksmithing weapons for those who had their weapons confiscated by the Ugandan authorities. As the authorities became more effective at enforcing the law and other tribes became distrustful of the Iks' double agentry, these means of support were also lost. The Ik were eventually forced into constant leisureless, subsistance-level food gathering as their last recourse for survival.

The Ik demonstrate that the ultimate human goal, survival, is not always a pretty one. The cumulative effect of the Iks' failures at developing a viable economy in inadequate circumstances was quite dramatic. It literally destroyed the simple human tribal bonds, the caring sense of community. Because they had been starving to death for nearly a generation, the Ik took drastic measures to ensure the tribe's continuity. Whether they realized they were making the choice or not, they eventually began to reduce the tribe's numbers. They let their elders die simply by not feeding them and not carrying them from place to place as the tribe foraged for food. When that was no longer enough, they reasoned, "Why feed the young? If they can't look after themselves, they won't survive anyway." So only those who were healthy and children over three who could forage for themselves survived. With tribal bonds thus disintegrating, common family bonds fell. Husbands and wives abandoned each other when they became ill or disabled; women bore children begrudgingly and raised them with no enthusiasm.

We often tell ourselves that the luxuries of generosity, kindness, compassion, affection, and love are basic to human nature; but the Ik illustrate that when one's basic survival needs are threatened, these humanizing qualities may eventually be stripped away, leaving a human society shorn of all needs save one—the basic physiological need to survive!

The story of the Iks' changing lifestyle illustrates how the suggestions of Miller and Sjoberg and Maslow can fit together to form a pyramid of human needs and life-styles (see Figure 6.2). Given the complexity of human needs, each dimension or side of the pyramid possess many different purposes and meanings. Work may be a curse or a blessing. When done only from necessity, it can be a hard and demanding activity that satisfies our basic needs for food and shelter but saps our energy, time, and talents with little return. Over a long period of time, this form of work can damage or destroy our abilities to love and respect ourselves and others.

At a higher level, work can provide us with a sense of esteem,

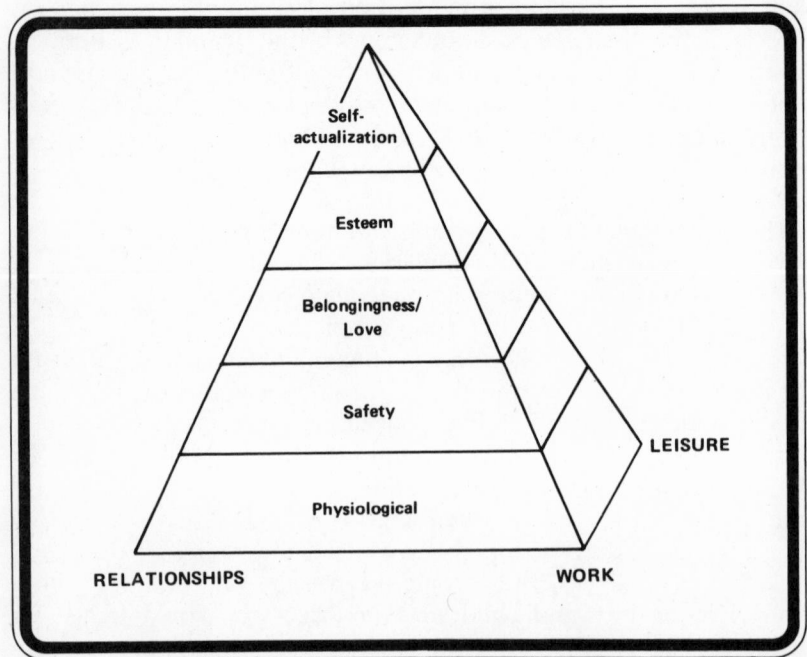

Figure 6.2   *The Life-Style Pyramid (adapted from Miller and Sjoberg, 1973, and Maslow, 1954)*

accomplishment, and competence when we share a sense of recognition for our talents and a feeling of belonging in the workplace. At its best, work can be a blessing when it provides us with opportunities for creativity, self-expression, and the full utilization of our talents and ambitions.

Our leisure activities also fit Maslow's framework. At one extreme leisure may be defined simply as escape from the demands of work. This kind of leisure is characterized by passivity, lack of obligation, avoidance of effort, and willingness to be entertained or to be diverted by something or someone. An example would be the person in front of the TV who is too tired to move. This person is a spectator and not a participant. We may feel guilty about this form of leisure if we believe that idleness is frivolous.

Leisure can also be used in a more purposeful way for recreation, revitalization, or self-juvenation. Using leisure in this way means participating in some activity that is different from work. Unlike the first form of leisure—that of work avoidance and passivity—this form of leisure supports the work effort by rekindling lost energies through active involvement in free-time activities.

The third, or classical, view of leisure is not dependent upon any notion of work. Here leisure is an ideal pursued for the sake or enjoyment of an activity itself. Leisure in this sense is not concerned with what is produced, accomplished, or avoided, but in what is being experienced at the moment. This form of leisure may occur in any context, including a work setting. The action occurs solely for the sake of positive experience derived from participating in the activity. A celebration is an example of this type of leisure experienced to its fullest.

The third side of the life-style pyramid is relationships. Like work and leisure, our relationships with other people may have different meanings depending upon the needs we are attempting to satisfy through contact with others. At one level a relationship may have a basic yet essential utilitarian function. Through a relationship between a man and a woman procreation occurs and in this manner life is initiated and extended. At other points, our relationships may fill our needs to be protected from harm, to be valued and recognized, to experience belongingness, to lead, and to support and assist. In relationships we thus have opportunities to get to know ourselves better and find these parts of ourselves and others that we cherish and feel good about. Finally, at their best, most intimate self-actualizing relationships are similar to leisure since they may be experienced and maintained for no other purpose than the enjoyment of being with another person. A self-fulfilling intimate relationship with a friend or lover is often defined in this way.

The life-style pyramid thus helps us connect the various aspects of our lives at any point in time and provides us with a general means of looking at our needs for growth both in and out of work. As with all forms personal development, our growth on the pyramid can be charted both upwardly and around the pyramid. At different points in your life you may notice that you feel more fulfilled in some areas of the pyramid than you do in others. For example, you may find meaning and satisfaction in your work but be struggling to find satisfaction and purpose in your relationship and leisure pursuits. Having the awareness of areas where you can continue to grow may help you identify new courses of action to take to make your relationships and leisure activities more satisfying and your life experiences more complete. When viewed as a tool for self-understanding, the life-style pyramid helps us pull together our life needs and life-style into a meaningful and dynamic whole.

What area of your life-style provides you with the greatest sense of fulfillment? Where do you feel a need to grow? The Explorations in Life-style choice activities found in Appendix A have been designed to help you answer these questions. After reading this chapter, you may wish to complete one or two of the activities so you can use your current life situation as a guide in examining your future career possibilities.

FOUR BASIC CAREER PLANNING QUESTIONS

In her book on career planning, Celia Denues pointed out that, "To know where you want to go, you must know where you are and who you are." It is clear from her observation that the best place to start the occupation exploration process is with yourself, with your needs and preferences. So, let's start with questions about you, and then move to an exploration of how your career goals can be matched with the rewards and demands of particular occupations. In doing so, we will identify four questions that you will need to answer as you chart your current and future career paths. You need not worry about answering them just yet. We're simply going to identify them now and talk about their importance. Worksheets are provided at the end of the chapter for you to use in the actual process of gathering occupational information.

Who are you?

In previous chapters, we identified some of your occupational interests and abilities and applied John Holland's worker personality schema to college majors and occupations. Thus, you already have information about occupations to consider. Let's take your self knowledge a bit further, however, and explore a broader question.

How do you want to live?

Assuming that you had at least fourteen hours a day, seven days a week, to live the kind of life you most prefer, how much of your time would you invest on the three different sides of the life-style pyramid? Granted, the amount of time you would spend at these different activities would vary from day to day. It is nonetheless important to begin judging your time preferences early in the occupational search process so you can have some general guidelines for evaluating the occupations you explore.

Where do you want to live?

How you live is influenced by where you live. Some occupations are concentrated in specific areas of the country. Consequently, your geographic preferences may limit the occupations you consider. Other factors you may want to consider are the type of climate you most prefer, the size of community you would like to live in, and its cultural and recreational features. If you prefer first-run plays and art museums, you're not apt to be happy in an occupation that takes you out into the hinterlands.

What will you do for a living?

Once you have pulled together some of your life-style preferences, you can begin to identify the more specific rewards and demands that will help to make an occupation suit your goals and plans. For any occupation you consider, it will be helpful to come up with a description of its duties and rewards, including the amount of flexibility it provides and the level of responsibility it requires. Given what we said earlier about the stresses of jobs at different levels, it will also be useful to know how much of your time you will average on the job each week. On the rewards side of the ledger, it will be important to know what the occupation provides in terms of salary ranges, security, fringe benefits, vacation time, opportunities for advancement, and physical surroundings. Since very few of us work by ourselves, the people you will be associated with will be an important ingredient in your work-a-day world. As you explore an occupation ask yourself, "What are people who choose this occupation like?" "Do I share many interests and values in common with them? If I do not, how will I deal with my differences?"

Finally, you will need to know what type of educational and training experiences are required in order to successfully enter and advance in an occupation. Related to this, you will need to carefully consider your abilities, resources and opportunities, as well as how willing you are to invest your time, energy, and money in meeting these requirements.

By the time you have finished the process of gathering occupational information, you should be able to answer most of these questions in considerable detail. If you can, the odds are that, in addition to knowing who you are and where you are in the career planning process, you will also know where you want to go.

FINDING THE FACTS

Four major questions have been identified whose answers are needed in exploring the world of work: "Who am. I?", "How do I want to live?", "Where will I live?", and "What will I do to make a living?" Keeping these questions in mind as guidelines, your next task is to identify resources for obtaining occupational information. You will need to know what literature to read, which places to visit, and who to talk to. How thorough you can be in the occupational exploration process will depend upon how much time you have to invest in the process, and the kinds of resources that are available to you in your community.

Printed Materials

The easiest place to start is with two of the original "three r's," reading and writing. Most libraries and high school or college counseling offices contain books and pamphlets on different fields. Probably the most frequently used resource is the *Occupational Outlook Handbook*. Published yearly by the U. S. Department of Labor, the *Occupational Outlook Handbook* contains general occupational projections for the country as a whole, as well as information about some 300 occupations arranged by their common characteristics. Each occupation is described in terms of the nature of the work, place of employment, training and qualifications for advancement, employment outlook, earnings, and working conditions. Addresses are also provided for trade associations and state employment agencies that you can visit or correspond with to obtain additional information. Addresses of organizations are also provided for persons with special interests and needs such as women, the physically impaired, youth, and older workers.

The *Occupational Outlook Handbook in Brief* is a shortened version of the *Occupational Outlook Handbook* and provides a capsule summary of labor trends across the country and in specific occupations. Other helpful general source books include *What Can I Be? A Guide to 525 Liberal Arts and Business Careers*, the *Encyclopedia of Careers*, *Occupational Briefs*, *A Guide to Careers Through College Majors*, *Your College Degree*, the *College Placement Annual*, *Career Guide to Professional Associations*, and *National Trade and Professional Associations of the United States and Canada and Labor Unions*. Periodicals that you may find useful include *Changing Times*, *Glamour* magazine, *MS*, the *Journal of College Placement*, *Career World*, *Mademoiselle*, and two government publications, the *Monthly Labor Review* and *Occupational Outlook Quarterly*.

People Resources

The information you obtain from printed materials will really come to life when you take the time to talk with people about their jobs, observe them at their work, or read autobiographical sketches of people in different professions. The book, *Working*, by Studs Terkel or the *Vocational Biographies* series (published by Vocational Biographies, Inc., Sauk Center, Minnesota 56378), provide excellent sketches of people in different occupations.

Some of the students we have counseled express dismay at our suggestion that they talk with people about their work. They commonly say that they do not know anyone in the field they are considering, and believe that if they found such a person, that he or she wouldn't want to talk to them. A bit of detective work will solve the first problem, and a bit of self-confidence the other.

Let's start with the detective work. Suppose you were interested in talking to an automotive insurance claims adjuster who happens to be a woman. We've specified the person's sex because gender may be important to a female student who believes that the field provides limited opportunities for women. If you know a female claims adjuster, you're in luck. All you need to do is call her to set up a visit. However, let's make the problem more complex and assume you don't know such a person. One simple way of locating a female claims adjuster would be to look through the telephone yellow pages section on "insurance companies." Each insurance company will list its claims adjustment centers so all you need to do is call several companies and ask if they have a female auto claims adjuster that you can talk to. If a company doesn't have one, you might ask the person on the other end if they know of a company that does. Your school or college placement officer may also be able to help you by providing the names of alumni in your area who would be willing to help you in your search.

Another way of approaching the problem would be to develop your own informational network. Stanley Milgram, a social psychologist, believes that we can contact anybody in the world with from five to eight phone calls, even if we don't know the person. All we need to do is come up with a list of qualities the person must possess, including such characteristics as sex, place of residence, and occupation, and then begin to plan a strategy for contacting that person. For example, if I wanted to contact a female claims adjuster in Boise, Idaho, I might start calling relatives or friends who live in or have visited Boise to get their ideas about who I could contact in Boise. Or, I might call my family's insurance agent to solicit his or her ideas about who to contact. I would then call the persons that my local resources suggest, tell them who I was looking for and, using their advice, whittle my search down a bit further. Milgram suggests that by the time you have made five such phone calls, you should be in touch with the woman claims adjuster from Boise. Needless to say, your task will be easier if you are looking for a person in the community where you live. But, in either case, the basic method of investigation remains the same.

② The second problem, that of overcoming your reservations on talking to people about their professions, also has several solutions. Although many students believe that professional people are too busy to bother with students, our experience proves otherwise. Most people love to talk about what they do. Sure, there will be some individuals who can't be bothered talking about themselves. If you are persistant, however, and effectively use your network of friends and relatives, the odds are that you will be able to locate several people willing to spend an hour or two discussing their work with you. We've also found that many alumni of our university are willing to have students spend a day observing them at their work. Thus, the problem of locating willing persons may not really be a problem at all.

Students often stumble in this process because they don't have a clear set of questions they want answered. This again speaks to the need of clarifying your life-style needs, and using them as a framework for asking others about their life-styles. If you are anxious about what to ask and how to ask it, you may want to develop a list of specific questions and find a friend or relative to help you through a practice interview. In that way you can refine your questions, overcome some of your fears, and sharpen your interviewing skills.

One final point. If you decide to use the interviewing for information approach, remember to send each person you interview a thank you note.

Visiting–Volunteering–Working

Reading about an occupation or talking with people about it are two important ways of gathering occupational information. If you really want to explore an occupation, however, we encourage you to try to get some "hands on" opportunities in it. Some corporations provide tours for the public to explain how they produce their products. You may be able to arrange a tour in a setting that employs persons in the field you are interested in.

If you have the time and the motivation, you may be able to persuade an employer to allow you to work as a voluntary apprentice for one or several days as a way of exploring an occupation and your reactions to it. It may also be possible to find part-time or summer work in the field or in related fields. Finally, you can take advantage of the cooperative education, internship, and externship opportunities that may be available on your campus. Through such programs, you will be able to work part-time in settings that relate to your degree program. An advantage of this, as well as any of the other "hands on" opportunities you can participate in, is that in addition to being able to gather occupational information, you will be building skills for securing a full-time job at graduation. In fact, many employers use volunteer and internship programs to evaluate and groom potential employees.

EVALUATING OCCUPATIONAL INFORMATION

"Caution! Occupational information may be hazardous to your career." As farfetched as this statement may seem, there is some truth to it. Hidden biases may be conveyed in occupational information. Labor projections are based on two premises—no war and no depression. Optimistic projections from some sources may represent an attempt to sell a field that is unstable. Be careful that your enthusiasm for a field that has "opportunities for well-qualified applicants" does not blind you to its disadvantages. (Every field has some!)

We noted in the first chapter that, until recently, participation in the American economy was restricted for women and minorities, who have access to only a limited number of occupations. Because of their economic isolation, we find that a disproportionate number of women and blacks have traditionally been pushed to work in occupations that provide services to others such as teaching, nursing, and social services.

The salary structures for women and blacks working in these areas has historically been markedly different from those of white males. In 1977, for example, women comprised 42% of the national labor force, but received only 25% of the total earnings of American workers. The median salary for men during 1977 was $253 per week; the median salary for women was $156 per week. Because of these restrictive circumstances, the potential role models for students who are female and/or Black, and are interested in fields that have been traditionally open to men, are very few in number.

The sexual, ethnic, and racial biases that are associated with economic discrimination are subtly conveyed in many sources of occupational information. Pictures that show a person of a particular group working at a given profession tend to project the image that the field is for them only, thus confirming widespread and inaccurate beliefs about who should work where. This does not imply that the people who create informational materials want to exclude some groups from certain occupations. However, it does demonstrate how the cultural stereotyping process has served to restrict the availability of potential role models for individuals wishing to explore certain fields. This can be discouraging, if you let it.

Be *thorough*, use a wide variety of informational resources. Explore groups of related occupations and their different levels. Make sure the information you obtain is *current*. Check the date of each publication you read and compare the information it contains against the information from the most recent edition of the *Occupational Outlook Handbook*. Lastly, make sure that the information is *accurate* (and reasonably objective) by noting how the information was gathered, how many people were surveyed to obtain it, and who published it. Also, compare national trends against local trends. You may find that while a field is tight locally it may be more open in other areas of the country.

Finally, use the activities that follow to evaluate the information you have gathered in light of your life-style needs and preferences.

IDEAL JOB DESCRIPTION

To avoid the feeling of exploring occupations without a sense of direction or purpose, it will be helpful to have your own needs and priorities in mind prior to gathering occupational information. This activity is designed to help accomplish that objective.

Imagine that you have the opportunity to create your ideal job; one that fits the unique you and the way you want to live. Take several sheets of paper, and using the information you have gathered about yourself so far, create a written sketch of the way you would most like to spend your life in the future. In doing so, try to answer the four basic career planning questions identified in this chapter.

First, *Who are you?* Start with the life stage that is most descriptive of where you are currently. What are the needs and pressures that affect you right now? How are you dealing with them? What choices will you be making during the next five years?

Next, recall the three Holland worker trait types that seemed most descriptive of you on the self-assessment activities found in the appendix of the text. Identify at least three interests and skills related to your code types that you would like to express through work. You may wish to take an interest and a skill from each of the three types, or you may pick three from one type. Other possible ways of combining types, interests and skills are also possible, depending on your own preferences. Explain in several sentences why you selected these interests and skills and how they fit into your career objectives.

Identify three values from the value analysis activity (found at the end of Chapter 5) that you want to express at work. Briefly explain the reasons you selected these three values and discuss their implications for your future.

Consider the type and amount of responsibility you want to take for decision making and supervision at work, and the effect it will have on the level at which you choose to work. Refer to Cosgrave's cube in Chapter 5 for more information about the different levels of responsibility.

The second question you will need to consider in developing your ideal job description is, *How do I want to live?* What is your preferred life-style? How would you ideally like to balance the time you spend at work, at leisure and recreation, and with family and friends? What kinds of things do you enjoy doing outside of work? What important needs will you be meeting through those activities? What salary will you need to support your life-style?

Third, ask yourself, *Where do I want to live?* If you have a geographic preference, state it and explain what makes it ideal for you.

Fourth, and finally, answer the question, *What will I be doing for a living?* Avoid giving your job description a title such as accountant or nurse, especially if you already have an idea about what you want to do. Try to look at the ideas you are including from a fresh perspective; make it a description of you, doing what you want to do (and not doing what you don't want to do), rather than a decription of a job that you think is realistic and available. Make the component activities, pleasures and problems clear and identifiable so that you may discover fields or settings where they might be used.

STRATEGIES FOR GATHERING INFORMATION

When you have completed your description of your ideal job, select at least two occupations that you would like to explore in depth. Be sure they are consistent with your three-letter code on the self-assessment activities in Appendix B. Write the titles of the occupations in the spaces provided on the pages that follow and try to identify the informational resources you will draw upon while exploring each occupation. You may wish to write to some professional associations for information. Addresses for a number of professional organizations are found in Appendix D. It will also be helpful to indicate when you plan on using those resources.

After you have identified the resources you will use to explore each occupation, turn to the *P.L.A.C.E. activity* for guidelines on how to pull together in a clear and simple manner, the information you have gathered about the different occupations. By comparing your ideal job description with information about specific occupations from the *P.L.A.C.E. activity* you will begin to sense which of the occupations you are considering are most consistent with your needs and preferences.

Occupation _____

I will *read* the following materials about this occupation by _____
(date)

A. _____

B. _____

C. _____

I will *talk* to the following person about this occupation by _____
(date)

A. _____

B. _____

C. _____

I will *visit* the following places who employ persons in this occupation

by _____
(date)

A. _____

B. _____

C. _____

If possible, I will *volunteer* some time to work along side of someone

in this occupation. I will do so by _____.
(date)

The person I will contact to see about volunteer opportunities is:

_____

Occupation _____

I will *read* the following materials about this occupation by _____
                                                          (date)

A. _____

B. _____

C. _____

I will *talk* to the following person about this occupation by _____
                                                          (date)

A. _____

B. _____

C. _____

I will *visit* the following places who employ persons in this occupation

by _____
                    (date)

A. _____

B. _____

C. _____

If possible, I will *volunteer* some time to work along side of someone

in this occupation. I will do so by _____
                                          (date)

The person I will contact to see about volunteer opportunities is:

_____

Occupation _____

I will *read* the following materials about this occupation by _____
                                                                    (date)

A. _____

B. _____

C. _____

I will *talk* to the following person about this occupation by _____
                                                                    (date)
A. _____

B. _____

C. _____

I will *visit* the following places who employ persons in this occupation

by _____
                            (date)

A. _____

B. _____

C. _____

If possible, I will *volunteer* some time to work along side of someone

in this occupation. I will do so by _____.
                                                (date)

The person I will contact to see about volunteer opportunities is:

_____

P.L.A.C.E: A GUIDE FOR EXPLORING AND EVALUATING AN OCCUPATION

As you explore different occupations, it will be useful to have a way of organizing the information you gather so that the various alternatives can be individually assessed and compared with each other. This can be accomplished using the following format for organizing occupational information. This system requires that you look at each occupation in terms of its:

P. Position description including general duties, occupational level, and associated enterprises.

L. Location, including the geographical locale and the physical environment where you will be working.

A. Advancement opportunities and job security.

C. Conditions of employment including salary, benefits, hours, and special demands such as dress codes.

E. Entry requirements including required educational and training experiences.

The following work sheets are designed to help pull together the *P.L.A.C.E.* information about each occupation you explore, and to evaluate it in terms of how the occupation fits the requirements of your ideal job. Use the five *P.L.A.C.E.* boxes on the left side of the page to write notes about the occupation. The comments section can be used to jot down your reactions to the occupation's characteristics. In making your comments you may wish to focus on how the demands and rewards of the occupation will affect your leisure–recreation and kinship–friendship pursuits. You can indicate how much the occupation appeals to you by circling 1, 2, or 3, in the box across from each characteristic of the occupation.

Circle 3 if the occupation has a definite or strong appeal to you.

Circle 2 if it has a moderate amount of appeal to you.

Circle 1 if it has little appeal to you.

Circle 0 if it has equally appealing positive and negative qualities or if you are indifferent to it.

Circle −1 if that is you are turned off in a small way by the occupation.

Circle −2 if its negative qualities turn you off in a moderate way.

Circle −3 if its negative qualities completely turn you off.

After you have rated the occupation in each of the five areas, total the circled numbers and write the figure you obtained in the box at the bottom of the page next to where it says, "total rating." This score, which can be positive or negative, will provide you with a sense of the occupation's overall appeal to you. You can later compare this figure with the totals you obtain from rating other occupations to get an idea about which of the occupations you have explored most appeals to you.

OCCUPATION EVALUATION WORKSHEET

Position title _____

Characteristics of the occupation	Comments	Rating
P. Position description *Notes:*		-3 -2 -1 0 1 2 3
L. Location *Notes:*		-3 -2 -1 0 1 2 3
A. Advancement opportunities *Notes:*		-3 -2 -1 0 1 2 3
C. Conditions of employment *Notes:*		-3 -2 -1 0 1 2 3
E. Entry requirements *Notes:*		-3 -2 -1 0 1 2 3

Total rating =

A PLACE FOR YOUR VALUES

We have previously explored how your personal values have emerged and changed over time and how they influence your decisions. This activity provides you with an opportunity to examine how well the different occupations you are currently exploring match your values. In completing the activity, you will be asked to identify values and to use them as a criteria for assessing occupations. Worksheets are provided for comparing up to three occupations.

Once you have learned how to use this technique, you may find it helpful to use it in making other career decisions, such as selecting from among job possibilities or deciding on a promotion. The same approach can be used in other areas of your life, including decisions about a major purchase, about where you will live, or about where you will go on vacation. The only information you will need for each of these decisions is a list of your values and a list of alternative choices.

The format for this activity is basically the same as that of the P.L.A.C.E. activity except that instead of looking at occupations in terms of position location, and so-on, you will be using your values as your criteria. The activity involves three steps.

Step 1.   Identify your values

Read through the list of values provided below and put a check mark in the box next to those values that are *most important* to you— the values that you must have the opportunity to express if you are to be happy with your major or work.

The ideal job would have to . . .

☐ provide me with *achievement, recognition, status,* or approval from others.

☐ provide me with opportunities and time to appreciate *beauty* in people, art, and nature.

☐ provide me with *challenging opportunities* to use my creativity, training, intelligence, and talents.

☐ provide me with opportunities to experience *good health physically* and *mentally* by being free of anxiety and stress.

☐ provide me with an opportunity to *improve my financial position* significantly.

☐ provide me with *independence* to be free to do my own thing, independently of others.

☐ provide me with time to devote to *close personal relationships* with my peers and family.

☐ provide me with an opportunity to work in settings that agree with my *moral* or *religious standards.*

☐ provide me with time for *pleasure* and *fun.*

☐ provide me with opportunities to *influence* or *control* the activities of others.

☐ provide me with *security* and *safety* from unexpected or unpleasant change.

☐ provide me with opportunities for *personal development* by using my talents and interests; support me in my efforts to become more well rounded as a person.

☐ provide me with opportunities to be of *service* to others.

Step 2.   List your values

From each of the values you have checked, write down the under-lined words as those being most important to you, in the column labeled "My most important values are" on page 128. List one value in each box.

Step 3.   Indicate the occupation being considered

Write the title of the occupation you are considering in the space provided at the top of the page.

Step 4.   Gather information about the occupation

Use the same procedures you used in the P.L.A.C.E. activity for gathering information about an occupation. Write your observations in the comments section of the grid.

Step 5.   Rating the occupation

Rate the occupation according to the following scale. Circle the appropriate rating next to each value.

Circle 3 if the occupation is very consistent with your value.

Circle 2 if the occupation is generally consistent with your value.

Circle 1 if the occupation is somewhat consistent with your value.

Circle 0 if the occupation has some qualities that are consistent with your values and some that are not.

Circle − 1 if the occupation is somewhat inconsistent with your value.

Circle − 2 if the occupation is generally inconsistent with your value.

Circle − 3 if the occupation is very inconsistent with your value.

Step 6.   Total Value Rating

After you have rated the occupation for each of the values, total the circled numbers and write the figure you obtained in the space labeled "Total rating." (In calculating your totals remember that a minus is always subtracted from a plus.) This score, which can be positive or negative, will provide you with a sense of the occupation's value to you. You can later compare this figure with the totals you obtain from rating other occupations to get a clear idea about which of the occupations that you have explored has most appeal to you.

OCCUPATION EVALUATION WORKSHEET—VALUES

Occupation _____

My most important values are	Comments	Rating
		-3 -2 -1 0 1 2 3
		-3 -2 -1 0 1 2 3
		-3 -2 -1 0 1 2 3
		-3 -2 -1 0 1 2 3
		-3 -2 -1 0 1 2 3
		-3 -2 -1 0 1 2 3
		-3 -2 -1 0 1 2 3

Total rating =

REFERENCES

Denues, C. *Career Perspective: Your Choice of Work.* Worthington, Ohio: Charles D. Jones Publishing Co., 1972.

Maslow, A. *Motivation and Personality.* New York: Harper, 1954.

Milgram, S. The Small World Problem. *Psychology Today,* 1967, *1,* 62–67.

Miller, P. J. and **Sjoberg, G.** Urban Middle-Class Lifestyles in Transition. *Journal of Applied Behavioral Sciences,* 1973, *9,* Nos. 2/3 pp. 144–162.

Turnbull, Colin M. *The Mountain People,* New York: Simon and Schuster, 1973.

chapter 7

Finding a Job is a Job!

When nothing else seems to help, I go and watch the stone cutter hammering away at his rock, perhaps a hundred times without a crack showing in it. Yet on the hundred-and-first blow the rock will split in two, and I know that it was not only that blow which split it, but all that had gone before.

Jacob A. Riis

Most students wait until graduation is rapidly approaching before they begin a job campaign. Although they've had part-time and summer jobs, they may be fearful about how to approach real work, something that they may be doing for the rest of their lives. While it is true that a temporary job may involve less personal investment than a long-term one, there are some important similarities between the two. If you recognize and capitalize on these similarities the odds are that you will be more satisfied in pursuing your career goals.

PROFITING FROM EXPERIENCE

Temporary and long-term work share common opportunities to learn and to demonstrate new skills. The newspaper route you may have had when you were younger provided chances to learn how to deal with the public, to sell a product, to manage money, and to organize time around work tasks. Think about the rainy days when you were forced to demonstrate perseverence and "intestinal fortitude!"

As we mentioned in the preceding chapter, it is wise to investigate and consider any appropriate volunteer or cooperative education experiences that are available through your college. Such experiences are a rich source of occupational information. They provide opportunities to confirm and develop your skills, and to make contact with potential employers.

Since the skills you demonstrate in temporary jobs can be applied to long-term settings, it helps to catalog your past work experiences. Include in your list any involvements you have in student and community organizations while you are in school. Making this list will help you recall and pull together the bits and pieces of your work related experiences. A simple way of doing this would be to use an index card such as the one shown below to record each of your learning experiences or the personal skills inventory provided at the end of this chapter. Catalog past jobs and begin now to keep a current record of new experiences as they occur.

Temporary and long-term jobs also involve a similar job search process. Unless you worked in your family's business, you had to do some job campaigning to locate any employment you have held.

Generally speaking, the major difference between campaigning for temporary and more permanent jobs is that since a greater commitment is being made, the latter usually requires a longer and more formalized procedure. Resumes must be prepared, cover letters transmitted, and formal interviews conducted. If you wait until near

Activity _____

Place (address) _____

Dates _____ Supervisor _____

Salary (if any) _____

Description of duties:

Skills I demonstrated:

graduation to develop your formal job hunting skills, you will probably experience some distress about the process and feel rushed. It
is, after all, a new situation requiring development of new skills. We
believe that while practice may not make perfect, it does a lot to
create self-assurance, prevent mistakes, and relieve the anxiety of a
job campaign. Consequently, this chapter is written to help you learn
formal job search skills that can be used while applying for temporary
or volunteer work, as well as permanent jobs.

THE TRADITIONAL JOB CAMPAIGN

To conduct an effective job campaign you will need to answer four
questions:

What do I want to do?
When will I begin?
Where do I want to do it?
How will I go about getting it?

What Do I Want To Do?

Narrowing down and learning about the possible answers to this question has been your goal up to this point. Cornerstones of this decision are your personal qualities and your self-image. These include preferences, attitudes, beliefs, values, interests, and skills. You have expressed them in your work history, self-assessment activities, Holland code types, ideal job description, life-style preferences, daily decisions and interaction with others. They are affected in turn by your history, experience, decision and planning style, life stage, and choice of life-style. When it comes to making and implementing tentative commitments, attention must be paid to specific preferences such as: work location, environment and level, training and experience needed, and to the balance between what you must give to the job and what you get back. Many of these issues can be clarified by the search for occupational information and opportunities.

When Will I Begin?

This question has two parts: When do you want to start to work? and When will you begin your job campaign? Starting at the end first—a date for starting work—will allow you to plan time to conduct a thorough job campaign, one that will permit you to explore a variety of options under minimal time pressures. While there are no precise rules for how much time you may need to spend preparing for and conducting a job campaign, remember that planning ahead will produce better results. For example, if you are thinking about working at a national park for the summer, you might start writing away for information during the preceding fall. Then you have at least five months to explore your options and another five months to conduct a formal job search process.

Where Do I Want To Do It?

Having clarified a personal direction and decided how long you need to carry on your job campaign, you can begin the task of identifying and evaluating specific work opportunities. These opportunities can be identified in a variety of ways: friends and relatives, newspapers and trade journals, professional associations, offices, government and private employment services, and direct contact with employers. Take advantage of the placement office on your campus. Your placement officer can help you locate jobs, help you polish your written application materials and interviewing skills, and match you with employers who are recruiting students on your campus.

Once a list of potential employers has been generated, the actual task of job campaigning can be started. The traditional way of doing this involves preparing a resume that summarizes your background; then sending it with an accompanying cover letter to prospective employers with the hope of securing a follow-up interview. During the on-site interview, a mutual negotiation process occurs during which you and the employer balance your individual wants and needs against each other's aims and objectives. More will be said about this shortly.

A bit of preliminary research about each of the organizations you are thinking of contacting can help you present yourself (on paper and personally) in a way that stands out in a large pool of applicants. It can also boost your confidence and help you prepare for subsequent job interviews. Gather as much information as you can about the employers that interest you. Use company brochures, Dunn and Bradstreet Reports, public financial information (including salary information which is vital in negotiating employment conditions), and word of mouth insights from friends, family, your college advisor, and your placement officer. All of this gives you a picture of the firm's economic stability and its growth potential.

Most job applicants use a mass mailing procedure, sending the same resume and cover letter to all employers, regardless of how the companies differ. While this approach may have some success, it may not catch the employer's eye as effectively as a cover letter that shows you have done your homework and know about the employer's enterprise. The background information you have gathered to identify potential employers can be used to tailor your cover letter to the employer's needs. Although most students use the same resume with different cover letters for different employers, some attempt to create a cover letter and resume for each employer. There are no clear rules about this and we know of no evidence to support either approach. The best advice we can give you is to choose an approach that best suits your own style and the amount of time and money you are willing to spend in preparing your resume.

The knowledge you have about employers can also help in making decisions about whether or not to send out applications in the first place. After all, employees hire employers, too! In making such initial decisions, it is helpful to prepare a list of criteria for evaluating employers. Some criteria you may wish to use include: the size of the organization, its location, its history and image, its products or services, its administrative and promotional structure, its atmosphere and attitudes toward employees, and its future prospects. In short, the same requirements you would use to evaluate a full-time job. Specific guidelines for preparing a cover letter and resume are provided later in this chapter. You may also wish to use Richard Bolles' book, *Three Boxes of Life*, to identify other ways of locating employment information.

A Novel Approach to Job Campaigning   John Crystal and Richard Bolles have developed an alternative approach to the traditional job search just discussed. As with the traditional approach, they advocate that you start your job campaign by identifying the type of work you want to perform (the skills and interests you want to express through work). After you determine what you want to do, they suggest that you identify the specific geographic location where you want to live. You can do this by making up a list of criteria for your ideal living and working environment (size of the community, weather preferences, terrain, leisure and cultural opportunities), and then identifying the place or places that most closely match these criteria. Once you have decided upon a particular place, Crystal and Bolles suggest that you visit it to conduct a job campaign. The phone company can assist you in the early exploration process by sending you free copies of directories for communities that interest you. Directories are also available in many public libraries. The directories can be used to explore community resources and to identify and contact potential employers. Needless to say, this can be an expensive way to find a job. One way to offset the costs of job exploration, however, is to use the job campaign as a working vacation by visiting areas of interest during free time prior to a job search.

Crystal and his associates suggest that two steps be taken in contacting employers in your preferred environment. *The first step is to conduct a community survey*. This requires that you locate at least one work setting where your talents can be utilized and attempt to set up an information-gathering interview with the person who makes decisions about personnel in that setting. Such persons might include vice presidents, managers, and personnel directors but not clerks and receptionists who simply implement decisions. The information-gathering interview is used to explore in a personal way the atmosphere of the company, its plans for the future, and the specific needs of the employer. The idea is to gather and share information, *not* to secure a job. Remembering this can alleviate your anxieties about applying for a job and provide valuable insights into the organization. At the conclusion of the information-gathering interview you can ask your interviewee for the names of other individuals in similar positions who can be contacted for additional informational interviews. These persons are then contacted and interviewed in a similar manner until the entire community has been canvassed.

A thorough informational interviewing campaign will cover most of the employers who may have jobs of the type you wish to pursue. This can lead to two important outcomes: (1) you will know where the potential but hidden jobs are (Richard Irish suggests that up to 80 percent of the jobs in this country are hidden) and (2) you will know which companies offer the work atmosphere that most appeals to you. Having this knowledge, you can eliminate undesirable prospects and pursue more desirable ones.

⌐ *The second step in this process is to develop a prospectus to submit to desired employers.* The prospectus should include your observations of the positive aspects of the employer's setting, your projections of the employer's needs, and the special qualities you have to offer to fill those needs. In essence, you are writing your own job description—a contract that is open to mutual negotiation. After the employer has had time to read your prospectus, you should recontact him or her and set up an interview to present your case, a task that requires a considerable amount of self-confidence and sensitivity to others.

How Will I Go About Getting It?

The paper work process of conducting a job campaign traditionally has required that you prepare three documents: (1) a background resume, (2) a cover letter to accompany the resume, and (3) follow-up correspondence after the employment interview. Guidelines for each of these activities are provided in the paragraphs that follow.

CONTENTS OF A RESUME

Identifying Information.   Your name, address, and telephone number; possibly some of the items from your personal data. Both a permanent and temporary address may be included.

Personal Data.   An extension of the identifying information giving such vital statistics as age, height, weight, marital status, number of children, early background (if it is significant), hobbies and other activities. (Some of these things may be left out or deemphasized in circumstances where they may not be an asset.) The information is optional.

Job Objective.   The Job Objective identifies the responsibilities, challenges, and work activities that you wish to assume. Use job titles or descriptive phrases to specify the particular job or kind of job you are looking for. You may wish to state entry-level as well as long range goals. The *Dictionary of Occupational Titles* may be helpful in locating appropriate job titles, as well as in putting into words the range of duties sought.

Educational Backgrounds.   List of schools attended, dates, degrees, diplomas, and certificates with emphasis on highest level achieved and special training pertinent to your job objective.

Experience or Work History.   A summary of your work experience describing the nature of the work, job title, name of employer, and inclusive dates of employment. Work experience relevant to your job objective should be emphasized. Since most students have little, if any, relevant experience, it is important to list all summer, part-time jobs, and significant volunteer positions.

Military Record.   A brief statement of your service obligations, if any, or your experience if your tour of duty is completed. If your work history and your educational background were mostly military, then include your military experience and training under these previous headings.

References.   It is satisfactory to state simply that references will be supplied on request. However, if you are registered with a placement office and have a complete credential/job placement file, then reference should be made to the availability of your confidential data from that office, noting its full address and telephone number. If you are filling out an application, it may ask for 2 or 3 people who can be contacted as references. So, before beginning your job campaign identify those people, ask their permission to use their names, and obtain complete addresses and phone numbers.

Date, Statement of Availability.   These items are optional but it is desirable to date each resume as you distribute it and to mention when you are available for work.

Resume Suggestions[1]

1. Your resume should be confined to one page if possible. Very few college students have had enough experience to justify more than that. If you are one of those few, however, do not hesitate to use the space you need to tell your story, but do not go beyond two pages.

2. Experiment with the arrangement of headings, captions, and text so as to find the best total appearance and readability. Use capital letters and underlining sparingly. Use indentation as a means for identifying separate items. Organize material so that facts and categories can be found easily by the reader.

3. Balance the material on the page so that the total effect is pleasing to the eye. Leave sufficient margins so that the page does not look crowded. Fill the page, so as not to leave excessive space at the bottom.

4. Be consistent in the use of graphic display techniques. Do not use indentation in one section and underscoring in the next.

5. As you edit your material keep in mind your intended purpose. Eliminate unimportant details, and stress accomplishments you are proud of. Write and rewrite until you are satisfied that your descriptions are factual and positive statements of your experience, giving promise of potential and continued growth.

6. You may write in complete sentences or splinters of sentences as long as your meaning is clear. The test is whether your text is readable and understandable. Use simple words that convey exactly the meaning you intend. Use punctuation marks intelligently.

7. It is not necessary to use the first person pronoun unless the text does not make sense without it. Since you are writing about yourself, verbs will imply the "I" as the subject of your sentences. Use of the third person in referring to yourself is not acceptable unless it is contained in a quotation by another person.

8. Use present tense in referring to activities in which you are currently engaged, but anything previous to current activity must be referred to in the past tense.

9. Avoid the use of slang, professional jargon and cliches. Do not abbreviate. Employers who must take the time to interpret what you are saying will probably not bother.

---

1. Items 1–11 are taken from P. Dunphy (Ed.), *Career Development for the College Student*, Cranston, Rhode Island: The Carroll Press, 1973, pp. 89–90.

10. Consult a dictionary for correct spelling. Mistakes reflect on your education, and therefore your qualifications.

11. Before you type your final copy, have someone else react to it. Your family and friends or your school placement officer may be able to offer helpful suggestions. Consider your own reaction after setting it aside for a day or two. Would you hire the person described in this resume?

12. Have your resumes reproduced by a reputable copy or printing service.

13. When contacting an employer through the mail, *always* enclose a resume with a typed letter of introduction (see cover letter section of these guidelines).

TYPES OF RESUMES

Historical Format

If you believe that your most recent educational or work activity is your most important, place it first on your resume. Other experiences you have had would then be listed in their order of occurrence, starting with the most recent and ending with the most distant. Include the starting and ending dates to show how long you were involved in each educational or work activity.

This format is probably the most commonly used by job seekers, especially those with limited experience. Because of its logical sequence, it is easy to follow and allows the reader to rapidly trace your educational and work history.

Before you begin writing a historical resume, we would encourage you to jot down all of your educational and work experiences, then go back and select only those that are directly related to the job you are applying for. By doing so, you will avoid the common pitfall of losing the most significant aspects of your work history in a web of unessential facts and dates, and unimportant jobs.

Functional Format

The functional approach highlights the function or title of the positions you have held. In preparing this type of resume remember that your goal is to place your most significant work experience immediately before the employer. Job titles and specific duties are highlighted to support your qualifications for the job. While you should include names of employers and dates of employment with the descriptions, remember that they are secondary to the functions or positions you wish to emphasize.

This approach will be especially useful to you as you gain more experience because it allows you to highlight part-time, temporary, and volunteer work in your career field more effectively than you would be able to do with a historical resume.

Analytical Format

In the analytical approach you may emphasize particular vocational skills or specialized knowledge by grouping your background experiences according to their common features. Since you will be grouping your work experiences together according to their common qualities to demonstrate their applicability to a specific job, you will probably need to overlook historical sequence and specific job titles in prepariing an analytical resume.

Imaginative Format

The imaginative or creative format is probably the most difficult type of resume to prepare and the most risky to use. The general goal of this approach is to stand out from other applicants in some unique way because of the appearance of your resume. Applicants who use this type of resume may include aspects of the other approaches to resume preparation in new and unique ways, or they may create an entirely new format for highlighting their work history. Putting together a new style of presentation requires a considerable amount of planning and creative writing talent and a willingness to violate established norms. Common creative or dramatic methods of preparing imaginative resumes include unique graphic displays, headlines, colored paper or ink, and quotes from former employers or teachers.

Employers in the creative or artistic fields such as advertising, theater, and art are most apt to enjoy this type of resume. However, companies that are conservative in their orientation may decide that because you stand out so much they will leave you out. If you elect to try this type of resume, our best advice is to find out as much about each employer's style of conducting business as you can before you send them this type of resume.

The resumes that follow highlight the career path of a person, Mr. Larson, over time. As you read through each resume, notice how Mr. Larson uses the four different types of resumes described above to accomplish different job objectives. Also note how Mr. Larson emphasizes different aspects of his work history in each resume, thus demonstrating to employers that he has the skills and experience required to be successful in the position he is applying for.

EXAMPLES OF RESUMES

Historical Approach

Myron J. Larson
976 - 23rd Ave. N.E.
Minneapolis, Minnesota 55748

Job Objective: Forest Management

Education: University of Minnesota
            School of Forestry
            Graduated: March, 1941. BS degree
                        Major: General Forestry
                        Minor:

Experience:

July 1942 - April 1946   Naval Line Officer   U.S. Navy
            Mediterranean and Pacific Theatres. Served as deck officer on
            transport and instructor in landing craft. In charge of field
            work on a hydrographic convey in China.

January 1942 - July 1942   Asst. Supt. U.S.D.A. Bureau of Entomology
                             and Plant Quarantine
            In charge of field work-burberry eradication in Morrison County.
            Planned and supervised work of crew comprised of 30 men and
            3 foremen.

October 1941 - January 1942   Administrative Guard.   U.S. Forest Service.
            Cruised, scaled, marked timber, and supervised CCC crews while
            planting and fire fighting.

July 1941 - October 1941   Junior Foreman, CCC. U.S. Forest Service.
            Supervised CCC enrollees in all phases of general forestry
            work; cruising, planting, and fire fighting.

March 1941 - July 1941   Foreman and Asst. Supt. U.S.D.A. Bureau
                           of Entomology and Plant Quarantine.
            In charge of field work - burberry eradication in Grant County.

Hobbies: Hunting and Fishing

May 1946

Functional
Approach

Myron J. Larson
1608 - 2nd Ave. S.W.
Grand River, Minnesota

Job Objective: Administrator of forest management and wood procurement
program for paper producers.

Experience

Project Forester   State of Minnesota. Park Rapids, Bainerd, and Grand
River areas.

Furnished forest management service to private woodlot owners.
Services included planting, cruising, marking timber, developing
management plans and providing marketing information. Serviced
forest development programs and managed state forest land.

Administrative Guard/Jr. Foreman CCC   U.S. Forest Service Baldwin, Michigan

Supervised CCC enrollees in all phases of general forestry work.
Provided forest management services.

Asst. Superintendent   U.S.D.A. Bureau of Entomology and Plant Quarantine
Grant and Morrison Counties.

Planned and supervised work of 30 man crew completing field-barberry
eradication.

Naval Line Officer   U.S. Navy. Mediterranean and Pacific theatres.

In charge of hydrographic convey in China. Also served as deck officer
on transport and instructor in landing craft.

Education

B.S. Degree   University of Minnesota
Major: General Forestry   Minor:
Graduated: 1941

February 1956

Analytical
Approach

Myron J. Larson
Lake Road
Grand River, Minnesota

Job Objective: Public Affairs Director for paper producer.

Public Relations Activities: Served in leadership capacity for numerous
    local and state committees and councils promoting public awareness of
    forest resources, multiple use of forest lands, and conservation
    efforts taken by the wood products industry. Authored text, Forestry
    for Minnesota Schools, currently used in school system. Initiated
    and coordinated Minnesota Forest Industries public information program.

Governmental Relations: Lobbied at state and national level; have close
    working relationship with key legislative, and congressional personnel.
    Served on local, state, and national advisory committees and commissions
    for administration of national forests, state land exchange program,
    and state tree farm practices.

Forest Management and Wood Procurement: Developed forest management and
    wood procurement program; established tree nursery, recreation areas,
    land acquisition, cooperative research, and large-scale site preparation
    projects. Supervised staff of professional foresters, and managed
    wood procurement company.

Current Affiliations
    M.S. Salisbury Co. - Vice President and General Manager
    Minnesota Forest Industries Information Committee, Inc. - Chairman
    State Lend Exchange Review Board - member
    Superior National Forest Advisory Committee - member
    Grand River Chapter. Izaak Walton League of America - President
    Registered Lobbyist - Minnesota State Legislature

January 1973

Imaginative
Approach

Myron J. Larson

Graduate College of Forestry, University of Minnesota, 1941, B.S. degree in
Forestry. Worked as a supervisor of field crews Bureau of Entomology and
Plant Quarantine on Wheat Rust Control and as a Junior Foreman, C.C.C. and
administrative aide, U.S.F.S. Mainstee National Forest prior to entering the
service in 1942. After returning from service in the Navy in 1946 was em-
ployed by the State of Minnesota Division of Forestry as a Project Forester
stationed at Bemidji, Minnesota. From 1946 through 1956 assignments covered
Farm Forestry, Forest Management, Auxiliary Forest Supervisor, and Forest
Development programs in field offices at Park Rapids, Brainerd, and Grand
River areas. In 1956, left State employment and joined the Brown Paper
Company as Chief Forester, later becoming Woodlands Manager. Developed forest
management and wood procurement programs, established a tree nursery, recreation areas, land acquisition, cooperative research programs, large-scale site
preparation projects.

In 1973, became Public Affairs Director for Blandin and am currently serving
in this capacity.

Professional Accomplishments:

> Author - Forestry for Minnesota Schools first published in 1961,
>   revised 1972 and currently used in school system.
> Outstanding Forester Award 1962 - University of Minnesota School of
>   Forestry
> Member Superior National Forest Advisory Committee 1967-1976
> Member State Land Exchange Review Board 1968-1971
> Past Chairman, N.W. Chapter S.A.F.
> Past Chairman, State Keep Minnesota Green Committee
> Past Chairman, State Tree Farm Committee
> Past member, Institute of Agriculture, Forestry and Home Economics
>   Advisory Council
> Past member, Minnesota Association for Conservation Education
> Charter member Minnesota Forestry Association
> Member Forest Resources Committee, American Forest Institute
> Member Regional Communications Committee, American Forest Institute
> Society of American Foresters member since 1948

Miscellaneous

> Board Member Long Lake Conservation Center, Palisade, Minnesota
> Board Member Environmental Learning Center, Isabella Minnesota
> Past President, Grand River Chapter Izaak Walton League of America
> President, Forest Industries Information Committee (current)

                                        May 1979

THE COVER LETTER

An important rule of thumb for you to remember in corresponding with employers is that each time you send a resume to an employer it should be accompanied by a cover title. Your cover letter allows you to briefly introduce yourself to the employer by indicating why you are writing and what you can do for his or her organization. It briefly highlights your qualifications for a position and suggests a follow-up interview so you can more fully present your background experiences. Suggestions for preparing a cover letter and an example appear on the following pages. Typed cover letters always look more professional and present your resume in a better way than hand-written ones.

Correct Style for Application Letter
and Formula for Content

```
                                    Box 1945
                                    The Ohio State University
                                    Columbus, Ohio 43204
                                    Date
```

(allow 2 or 3 spaces)

```
Mr. George McCormick
Director of Personnel
American Manufacturing Company
124 North Evans Avenue
Chicago, Illinois 60645
```

Dear Mr. McCormick: (use name)

Opening Paragraph: State why you are writing, name the position or type of work for which you are applying, and mention how you heard of the opening.

Middle Paragraphs: Explain why you are interested in working for this employer and specify your reasons for desiring this type of work. If you have had experience, be sure to point out your particular achievements or other qualifications in this field or type of work.

Middle Paragraphs: Refer the reader to the attached application blank or personal data sheet, which gives a summary of your qualifications, or to whatever media you are using to illustrate your training, interests and experience.

Closing Paragraph: Have an appropriate closing to pave the way for the interview by asking for an appointment, by giving your phone number, or by offering some similar suggestion to facilitate an immediate and favorable reply. Ending your letter with a question encourages a reply.

```
                                    Very truly yours,
```

(always sign)

```
                                    Fred A. Summers
```

Enclosure   (if enclosing a resume, then note it)
            (top and bottom margins should be equal)

Application Letter

2707 South Standard Avenue
Columbus, Ohio 43214
Date

Ms. Jane R. Jones
Personnel Officer
Burke Technological Center
6401 Laughton Street
Los Angeles, California 90103

Dear Ms. Jones:

This morning's Los Angeles Times carried your advertisement for a "college student who is looking for a challenging and interesting summer position in a national park." With my educational background, practical experience and willingness to work in an interesting position that offers a real challenge, I am sure I can be of value to your service.

Next February I shall receive my Bachelor of Science degree from The Ohio State University, where I have majored in public recreation.

For the last six years I have worked at a variety of part-time jobs: waiter, customer service assistant, and assistant activities coordinator for the local YMCA. During the past two years, I have gained working experience which will be very valuable to your organization. Details of these jobs, my education, and other information may be found on the attached data sheet.

I know that I can fill the challenging position you have open, and I would appreciate an opportunity to meet with you at your convenience to discuss in detail my qualifications and future potential with your company. I may be reached every afternoon at (614) 267-9200, extension 32; or any evening at (614) 261-1282.

Sincerely yours,

Nancy T. Peterson

Enclosure

Follow-up Correspondence

After an interview, and especially after an on-site visit, a brief written reply to your interviewer or host is appropriate. This correspondence may include a thank you for the interview; a brief review of reactions to information provided to you; a response or follow-up to any specific requests made during the interview; and a request for additional information desired.

A major aim of this type of letter is to demonstrate your interest and initiative, and to keep your name before those who may be aware of future job openings. A sample letter is shown on page 149.

THE EMPLOYMENT INTERVIEW

Regardless of whether the traditional or nontraditional approach is used in establishing job leads, the step that follows is the same: the employment interview. The employment interview is an opportunity for you and an employer to meet, to exchange information, and to evaluate what each has to offer the other. As in any conversation between people, no two interviews are identical. Nevertheless, some common stages or components of an interview have been identified by the College Placement Council.[1]

The Opening

During the first few minutes of an interview, greetings and introductions will be made, handshakes exchanged and seats taken. Small talk may occur that appears to be unrelated to the business of securing employment. This stage will allow you to relax a little, to get accustomed to the interview situation, and to develop some initial impressions of the interviewer's style. This part of the interview is normally brief.

The Inquiry

A large number of questions are asked during this stage of the interview. The interviewer will try to obtain a clear understanding of your education, previous experience, achievements, and your short-term goals and long-term aspirations. He or she will use a large variety of questions to secure this information. Some may be very direct and require specific responses, while others may be more open-ended, providing you with an opportunity to emphasize your skills and interests. Although many questions may be directed to you

Example of a Follow-up Letter.

```
                                        815 N.E. 7th St.
                                        Hibbing, Minnesota
                                        Date


Ms. Jeanne Clarke
Associate Director of Personnel
Allied Products
Duluth, Minnesota

Dear Ms. Clarke:

    Thank you for the invitation and the opportunity to discuss the marketing
position available with your firm in Duluth.

    I was particularly impressed by the information you provided about the
in-service training opportunities with Allied Products. Likewise, your in-
centive and evaluation programs would provide the kind of salary, benefits,
and constructive feedback that are important to me at this point in my career.

    I have been giving a great deal of thought to the options you presented
for starting in a regional or division office. Since I prefer to live in a
larger metropolitan area, the division office assignment would be my first
choice. However, the range of duties to be performed at either type of office
is compatible with my experience and interest. I am attracted to both
opportunities.

    I understand that your recruiting process for this position will take an
additional two to three weeks. I look forward to hearing from you at that time.

                                        Sincerely yours,


                                        Maryann J. Olson
```

1. Adapted from The Audio Tape, "The Campus Interview—Are You Ready"? Used with permission of The College Placement Council.

during this phase of the interview, you should plan to ask some questions of your own as well. It is important for your own planning to clarify with who and for whom you will be working, what you may be expected to do, and where. Your questions will also demonstrate the research and thinking you have done about the job and the organization. A useful guide in choosing questions is not to ask questions that you yourself would be unwilling to answer.

The Matching

Matching occurs in two ways. The first screens you into a company by accentuating those skills, interests, and needs you possess that are consistent with what a potential position demands and provides. The second screens you out of a company by identifying factors that reflect differences between what you want and what the employer has to offer. Both types of matching are operating during the entire interview. The purpose of both is to recognize and project how your specific skills and goals might relate to specific job responsibilities and opportunities.

The Closing

Interviews may last for a few minutes or for several hours. Initial interviews will often be brief, with follow-up interviews taking considerably more time. Regardless, the main purpose of this last part of the interview is to specify what the next steps in the selection process are and who is to take the initiative. At times you may be asked to take additional placement tests, complete a physical examination, or return for further interviewing at another time, possibly with different people or at a different location. At other times, the interviewer may indicate that the selection procedure is complete and that you will be notified as soon as a decision is reached.

Often the person interviewing you is not solely responsible for determining who will be hired, and other candidates may still be waiting for an interview. When either of these situations exists, the status of your application cannot be decided until all the interviews are completed and the results of the selection process have been reviewed by everyone involved. Consequently, you may leave the interview with the feeling that you really do not know where you stand. The truth is that at the moment probably nobody else does either!

PREPARING FOR THE INTERVIEW

Information about yourself and the prospective employer is only a part of what is needed for effective interviewing. What you know about yourself and the employer needs to be confidently, clearly, and concisely communicated. These skills can best be enhanced through practice.

One way of practicing for an interview is to imagine that you are the interviewer. What kinds of questions would you ask of an applicant for a position in your organization? Frank S. Endicott, the former Director of Placement at Northwestern University, asked this question of recruiters for 92 companies. He found that the interviewers asked 50 common questions. Those questions are listed below.[2]

1. What are your long range and short range goals and objectives, when and why did you establish these goals and how are you preparing yourself to achieve them?
2. What specific goals, other than those related to your occupation, have you established for yourself for the next 10 years?
3. What do you see yourself doing five years from now?
4. What do you *really* want to do in life?
5. What are your long range career objectives?
6. How do you plan to achieve your career goals?
7. What are the most important rewards you expect in your business career?
8. What do you expect to be earning in five years?
9. Why did you choose the career for which you are preparing?
10. Which is more important to you, the money or the type of job?
11. What do you consider to be your greatest strengths and weaknesses?
12. How would you describe yourself?
13. How do you think a friend or professor who knows you well would describe you?
14. What motivates you to put forth your greatest effort?
15. How has your college experience prepared you for a business career?
16. Why should I hire you?
17. What qualifications do you have that make you think that you will be successful in business?

2. Reprinted by permission of Dr. Frank S. Endicott, Placement Office, Northwestern University, Evanston, Illinois.

18. How do you determine or evaluate success?
19. What do you think it takes to be successful in a company like ours?
20. In what ways do you think you can make a contribution to our company?
21. What qualities should a successful manager possess?
22. Describe the relationship that should exist between a supervisor and those reporting to him or her.
23. What two or three accomplishments have given you the most satisfaction? Why?
24. Describe your most rewarding college experience.
25. If you were hiring a graduate for this position, what qualities would you look for?
26. Why did you select your college or university?
27. What led you to choose your field of major study?
28. What college subjects did you like best? Why?
29. What college subjects did you like least? Why?
30. If you could do so, how would you plan your academic study differently? Why?
31. What changes would you make in your college or university? Why?
32. Do you have plans for continued study? An advanced degree?
33. Do you think that your grades are a good indication of your academic achievement?
34. What have you learned from participation in extra-curricula activities?
35. In what kind of a work environment are you most comfortable?
36. How do you work under pressure?
37. In what part-time or summer jobs have you been most interested? Why?
38. How would you describe the ideal job for you following graduation?
39. Why did you decide to seek a position with this company?
40. What do you know about our company?
41. What two or three things are most important to you in your job?
42. Are you seeking employment in a company of a certain size? Why?

43. What criteria are you using to evaluate the company for which you hope to work?

44. Do you have a geographical preference? Why?

45. Will you relocate? Does relocation bother you?

46. Are you willing to travel?

47. Are you willing to spend at least six months as a trainee?

48. Why do you think you might like to live in the community in which our company is located?

49. What major problem have you encountered and how did you deal with it?

50. What have you learned from your mistakes?

As you can see from Endicott's survey, employment interviewers cover a variety of topics during an interview ranging from your preparation for the job and commitment to it to your preferred lifestyle. As part of your preparation for the job interview, we would encourage you to read through the list of questions above and pick some that are difficult for you to answer as well as some that are easy and mentally rehearse your responses to them. You may wish to write the questions down or record them on tape. Respond to them out loud. Taping your answers will help you to hear how you present yourself to others. You may also find it helpful to sit down with one or two friends and practice interviewing one another. One person can serve as the employer. The other can observe the interview and critique your performance. When practicing for an interview, keep in mind that how something is said may be as important as the content. Your tone of voice, gestures, eye contact, and posture convey as much about you as what you say.

INTERVIEWING SUGGESTIONS

There are many factors that contribute to effective interviewing. Listed below are a few important tips:

Preparation

Know yourself. Have a clear understanding of your most prominent assets and goals and how these may be communicated. Know the organization. Be familiar with its products, priorities, and problems, and how your skills can contribute to its goals.

Physical Appearance

Let basic good taste determine how you dress. Wear clothing that you feel will represent you well and will convey an image of which you are proud. Above all, be neat and clean. Maintain a relaxed and alert posture. When listening or speaking to an interviewer, maintain eye contact.

Speaking Style

Be honest and be yourself. Speak clearly and with enthusiasm, and at a pace and volume that can be easily heard. Emphasize your strengths and be ready to support statements with examples. Be sure you understand the question before you answer it. Listen—pause— then respond. Ask questions. Remember that the interview is a two-way street. As you approach the interview, remember that the purpose of the interview is not to intimidate you or to put you through an embarrassing ordeal (although occasionally an interviewer will do that). The interview is the most efficient way for you and an employer to get to know each other in a short period of time. Recognize that you have qualities and attributes that will make you a valuable employee, and that an employer would not be meeting with you if he or she were not interested in the possibility of hiring you. Approaching an interview with confidence derived from an understanding of what may occur, from knowing yourself and being informed, and from prior practice will make the employment interview a valuable and rewarding experience.

WHEN A DETOUR IS NEEDED

Regardless of what job search method is used and how well we prepare ourselves for interviews, inexperience and an increasingly tight job market make it difficult to secure the ideal job on the first try. In fact, it appears that only a few students will secure their most preferred job right after they graduate. (Many of them later discover it is not their ideal job!) Statistics show that most people change jobs within two years of their first employment after college. This suggests that job shopping, like selecting a major, is a normal part of the ongoing process of career development beyond college. Consequently, it may help to alleviate job search pressures by putting aside the idea that one should achieve the ideal job standard on the first try. You should look at all jobs in terms of the opportunities for development they provide. To maximize your opportunities for growth in a tight job market, other work alternatives may have to be pursued, at least temporarily. The Vocational Contingency Planning (VCP) approach developed by Jeffrey Klienberg (1976) provides an alternative route and expanded opportunities when things do not work out as we hoped.

VCP is a useful back-up to the traditional and nontraditional approaches. Like the other approaches it starts with an identification of the specific work-related skills you possess. It is unlike the traditional approach, which emphasizes matching one's skills to specific job titles, and more like the nontraditional approach which looks at how specific skills can be transferred or utilized across a number of work settings and occupational levels.

The VCP strategy assumes that through employee turnover (retirement, death, advancement, and change) all occupations will in time have vacancies. VCP enables you to compete strongly for these openings when they become available. Essentially it offers three strategies for obtaining a primary occupational choice at some time in the future, even if the choice is currently inaccessible. The three alternative approaches are derived from classifying occupations in terms of level, field, and enterprise as was done on Cosgrove's World of Work Cube, and identifying the skills that various occupations share in common.

To illustrate, suppose your primary vocational choice, elementary public school teaching (a social occupation), were unavailable to you in the area where you want to work. VCP offers three options for using the social skills of a teacher:

Level Detour

You could seek a position in the teaching field at a level of responsibility below that of a full-fledged teacher, such as assistant or day care center aide.

Field Detour

You could seek work in an occupational field that relates in some significant way to the work of a teacher: textbook sales, audio-visual equipment maintenance, school security, or community liaison work. One way to identify field-related occupations is to list those occupations that a person in your primary occupation may have contact with during a normal day's activities.

Enterprise Detour

You could seek a position in nonpublic school settings, such as teaching in a private, parochial, or military school; tutoring; educational activities for a private firm; or volunteer work in community or government settings. This detour approach depends on locating other settings where the same type of work can be found.

All of these vocational detours allow you to:

1. Build up a positive work history with good, solid references in work activities related to your primary occupational goal.
2. Make personal contacts with those who might eventually be hiring you.
3. Pursue advanced study and training concurrently with the detour work.
4. Offer a richer repertoire of skills than is typically presented by the fresh-out-of-college applicant.
5. Prepare for the detour with a minimal amount of effort and time.
6. Engage in temporary work that will support you financially as you continue to pursue your primary goal.

VCP is not a panacea for achieving your primary occupational goal in a restrictive and deflated job market. It can increase the odds that you will eventually be able to attain your occupational goal, however, and that in the interim you will learn about your interests, your skills, and be exposed to many interesting job possibilities.

Three methods of job campaigning—traditional, nontraditional and contingency—were briefly presented in this chapter to illustrate the diverse ways a job search campaign may be conducted. Each of these approaches has advantages and disadvantages. Using aspects of each, you can develop a personal style that is most effective for you.

WHEN YOU ARE OUT OF WORK

Unfortunately, not everyone can be in the enviable position of looking for the next job while employed. At some time, after graduation, or due to circumstances in your life, you may find yourself unemployed. Here are some tips on how to cope with job hunting in that situation.

First and foremost, STAY ACTIVE! Keep yourself busy. Taking a part-time job will fill your time, make some money, and provide an opportunity to meet new people. Part-time or temporary work will also give you some time to spend in your job search—time to make contacts, write letters, interview, and make phone calls. Many employers are sympathetic to the plight of the young person looking for a first job. Saying that you are working part-time on a temporary basis while you look for a good job demonstrates that you are assertive and enterprising. And, if it is in a field that is related to your ultimate career goal, so much the better.

When you find yourself out of work, be prepared to pursue any and all leads that might land you a job. Letters, phone calls, and personal contact can all be important parts of your job search. As a general rule the job searcher will have to make thirty contacts with potential employers before getting a nibble. You can alleviate some of the anxiety by setting a goal of making thirty contacts in a month rather than feeling that you *must* have a job in two weeks. Decide to be an active agent in your job search, not passively dependent upon newspapers and employment agencies. Go out and look for a job— don't wait for a job to come your way.

PERSONAL SKILLS REVIEW

Throughout this text, we have stressed the importance of being able to identify and capitalize on the work-related skills you have acquired in order to effectively identify and pursue a career objective. We have also pointed out the benefits of a thorough skill assessment in developing a job search strategy; this will allow you to flexibly pursue a number of work alternatives in different work levels, fields, and enterprises.

Skill identification is especially important when you are conducting a job campaign. It allows you to put your best foot forward through correspondence and job interviews. Employers need to know that besides being interested in a job, as a potential employee you can demonstrate that you possess the appropriate skills for it!

We often think that the only skills and experiences that employers will be interested in are those that we can tie to formal educational, training, and work experience. Actually, we have had abundant opportunities in our leisure time and social pursuits to acquire solid skills that can be used in work settings. Being a member of a family, for example, can provide opportunities to observe how a mini-corporation (the family enterprise) manages its resources, utilizes lines of communication in decision making, and negotiates differences in style and opinions. Given this, it will be important to attend to the learning opportunities you have had on all sides of your life-style triangle. This can be done by using the card file suggested at the beginning of this chapter, or by identifying where and how you acquired the skills you noted that you possess on the self-assessment inventory provided in Appendix I. This approach can be especially helpful if you have had limited work experience or have "stopped out" from work. Other useful approaches to identifying your skills can be found in the books by Bolles and Haldane listed in the Resources section of this chapter. Regardless of how you approach the identification of your skills, it is important to be able to specify what the skill is, and where and when you learned it, so that you can accurately present your qualifications to employers.

You may conclude that you have some skills of significant quality and value which were learned in informal settings or were self-taught: cooking or child care in the home, bookkeeping for a club or group, running a local hospital benefit, photography for friends or a school paper, botany learned at city park classes. The origins of these skills may sound unprofessional but they can often be legitimized by imaginative additions, such as statistics, or examples or letters of recommendation. The hospital bazaar experience may look more professional diagramed on paper, detailing such things as your duties, number of people you supervised, and amounts of money handled. If your skill produces a portable product, bring a portfolio of your best work. If your product is not portable, it may show off well in photographs or drawings. If you have performed a service (cooking, child care, bookkeeping, photography) for individuals or groups in the community, or learned a skill from someone (the park director), ask for a letter of recommendation describing or confirming your skills.

The following *Personal Skills Review Inventory* is designed to help you identify and pull together all of the skills you have acquired. These include skills from your education or training and work experiences, as well as your leisure and recreation pursuits and your interactions with family and friends. The inventory requires that you clearly describe the specific skill that you wish to share with an employer and the context in which you acquired it. Examples are provided to stimulate your thinking. We also encourage you to go back through the skill items on the self-assessment inventory found in Appendix I to generate other skills for your list. If, for example, you indicated that you have a definite strong skill on item 1, "operating office machines,"—a conventional skill—you would try to identify on the personal skills inventory where and how you acquired that skill, and describe which machines you know how to operate.

PERSONAL SKILLS REVIEW INVENTORY

The skills

Learning context

Where I learned it

Describe the specific skills in terms of what it is, where you learned it, and when you learned it.

From Education–training

1. In my secretarial sciences curriculum at my technical college, I acquired specific skills in running a duplicating machine, a desk calculator, and a dictaphone. Other conventional skills that I acquired include . . . .

2. _____

3. _____

4. _____

From work experiences

1. In order to pay for my education, I worked part-time at night selling shoes. This offered me the opportunity to develop special and enterprising skills at meeting others, assisting them in meeting a specific need, and dealing with customer complaints. It also helped me acquire conventional skills in maintaining an inventory, exchanging money, and record keeping.

2. Finally, through this work I also learned how to keep a balanced budget to meet my own educational objectives. Thus, I am very familiar with the skill of setting priorities and long-range planning.

PERSONAL SKILLS REVIEW INVENTORY

Learning context

Where I learned it

The skills

Describe the specific skills in terms of what it is, where you learned it, and when you learned it.

3. _____

4. _____

From leisure–recreation pursuits

1. I like to fish, and during high school I learned how to tie flies for fishing, an artistic and realistic skill. I became so proficient at it that I soon was able to set up a profitable part-time business selling them. Through this experience I learned how to produce a quality product to meet a public demand, to manage a stock inventory, and to plan and manage a budget. I also learned how to effectively relate to customers. All of these are enterprising skills.

2. As captain of my YWCA baseball team, I learned how to support and encourage others, to give advice, and to present their views to people in authority (the coaches). These are primarily social skills.

3. _____

4. _____

From kinship–friendship activities

1. During the summer of my junior year in high school, both of my parents became quite ill for a month. Since I was the oldest child, I had to assume the responsibility for managing many household activities. Working with my relatives I learned how to plan schedules, project a family budget, negotiate difficult situations with others, and supervise the activities of others (my younger brother and sister). These managerial skills fall into the social and enterprising area.

2. _____

3. _____

4. _____

SOME USEFUL RESOURCES

Traditional Approaches

Brennan, L. D., Strand, S. and **Gruber, E. L.** *Resumes for Better Jobs.* New York: Monarch Press, 1973.

Corwen, L. *Your Resume: Key to a Better Job.* New York: Arco, 1976.

"How to Get a Job," Ohio Bureau of Employment Services, 1975.

Nutter, C. F. *The Resume Workbook.* (4th Ed.), Cranston, R.I.: Carroll Press, 1970.

Power, C. R. *Career Planning and Placement for the College Graduate of the 70's,* Kendall/Hunt, 1974.

Nontraditional Approaches

Bolles, R.N. *What Color Is Your Parachute?* Berkeley, California: Ten Speed Press, 1972.

Bolles, R.N. *The Three Boxes of Life.* Berkeley, California: Ten Speed Press, 1978.

Crystal, J.C. and **Bolles, R.N.** *Where Do I Go From Here With My Life?* New York: Seabury Press, 1974.

Haldane, B. *How to Make a Habit of Success.* Washington, D.C. Acropolis Books LTD, 1975.

Kleinberg, J.D. "Vocational Contingency Planning in a Recession." *The Vocational Guidance Quarterly,* 1976, 24 (4), pp. 366–367.

Irish, R.K. *Go Hire Yourself an Employer.* Garden City, N.Y.: Doubleday, 1973.

Lathrop, R. *Who's Hiring Who.* Berkeley, California: Ten Speed Press, 1977.

"Planning for Work,"[3] New York: *Catalyst,* undated.

"Your Job Campaign,"[3] New York: *Catalyst,* undated.

3. Resources dedicated to expanding employment opportunities for college-educated women who wish to combine career and family responsibilities. For more information contact: Catalyst, 14 East 60th Street, New York, New York, 10022.

8

Work Adjustment and Career Expansion

The life of a man involves daily the minute
predictions of the actions of other men.

Henry Sedgwick

We are all students of one another, constantly looking for clues about how others react to us. It is a survival mechanism, no doubt a part of us at birth, that helps us adapt to our environment.

Usually we are only dimly aware that we are "fortune telling," probably because our predictions are fairly accurate, and require little conscious thought. It is the unexpected event, the situation that we could not anticipate, that reminds us that our trust in others is based on their predictability. The change may be small—someone does not show up when they usually do—or it can be large, as when one travels to a new place. Our antennae go up, regardless, looking for new clues, new guidelines for dealing with the new situation. Until a new balance is established, we are likely to feel uneasy, even conflicted, about who we are and where we are.

The successful employee recognizes Sedgwick's truism opening this chapter. She or he realizes that the workplace is really a mini-society that sends out a constant stream of information about what is expected of its members, what the rules and limits are. Some of the rules are explicit, as in a job description or in a personnel hand-book. Many codes are hidden, however, revealed only in subtle patterns of behavior—in the workers' way of dressing, manner of speaking, topics of conversation, informal leadership patterns. All of these subtle cues fit together to create an organizational climate, a bond that maintains the stability of the work setting.

THE FIFTH SKILL: WORK ADJUSTMENT

The first four of the five skills mentioned earlier in this text should be second nature to you by now. All four—decision-making, self-assessment, information gathering and job search strategies—will be useful in job performance and expansion. In order to use them effectively to keep employed and grow with a job, a final skill—work adjustment—must be learned. The same people-reading skills discussed in reference to job interviews and job choice will be needed to deal with your employer's work environment and co-workers.

A 1975 survey of 5,213 employers by the Texas Advisory Council for Vocational Education serves to underscore the need for adaptive or social skills. The employers' responses to two questions are particularly illuminating: "What are your reasons for rejecting job applicants?" and "What are your reasons for hiring one applicant over another?" As is shown in Table 8.1, six out of the ten reasons for

TABLE 8.1

Employers' Reasons for Rejecting and Hiring Applicants*

Rejecting	Hiring
1. Little interest or poor reasons for wanting a job	1. Interest in job
2. Past history of job hopping	2. Ambitious
3. Inability of applicant to communicate during the job interview	3. Recommendations from previous employers
4. Health record	4. Health record
5. Immaturity (other than chronological age)	5. Maturity (other than chronological age)
6. Personal appearance	6. Personal appearance
7. Manners and mannerisms	7. Manners and mannerisms
8. Personality	8. Personality
9. Lack of job-related skills	9. Training background
10. Poorly filled out job application form	10. Previous work experience

* Adapted from *Qualities Employers Like, Dislike in Job Applicants,* Texas Advisory Counsel for Vocational Education, Austin, Texas, 1975.

rejecting an applicant were related to social and communication skills. Only after the effectiveness of the applicant's interpersonal skills and motivational level was established, did specific work skills assume priority. In looking at the reasons for termination of employees, Philip Dunphy (1973) reported a similar situation: "The vast majority of people who fail in jobs do so because they fail to relate well with other people."

Getting into a new environment begins with the initial task of observing and learning the hidden rules, pecking order, dress habits, conversational customs and individual roles (does your group of co-workers have a "gossip," a "snitch," a "mother hen," a "swinging single," a "scapegoat," or an informal leader?). A comfortable fit into a changing work group involves learning to interact pleasantly and tolerantly with all kinds of people, but it often requires much more than that. Many work situations require that each group member do part of a total job, which means group members must agree on goals and methods of operation and must be able to depend on each other. This requires working together, giving and taking directions, and sharing ideas and credit. Useful qualities in such a situation include patience, kindness, tolerance, discretion, tact, and when all of the above fail, the ability to handle conflict.

WHEN CONFLICT OCCURS

Despite the many commonalities that create a personality for a work environment, people differ greatly in the ways they approach their jobs. These differences are most likely to stand out when workers are under pressure, when their responsibilities are not clear, or when their personal expectations or needs are violated. All three situations often lead to conflict. Conflict situations offer an ideal opportunity to clarify personal differences and for team building. In fact, one reason people sometimes engage in conflict is to bring themselves closer together.

Regardless of the origin and content of the conflict, some simple guidelines can be followed to maximize its inherent opportunities for growth. First, do not let differences build up. Deal with them as they occur or you will run the risk of confusing several issues. Second, avoid personalizing the issue through placing blame or name calling. If the conflict is related to a colleague's behaviors, make sure that you keep the focus on the specific behavior, not the individual's personality. Notice, for example, how "When you extend your lunch hour without notifying me, I find myself feeling frustrated because I can't live up to my commitments. Please let me know when you're planning on being late in the future so I can schedule around it." differs from "You . . . You'll never learn. You made me miss my appointment. Wait 'til I tell your supervisor about it." Third, do your homework. Plan ahead and try to identify at least one positive alternative for correcting the situation, and plan on inviting other alternatives from the other person involved. That way you will have a better sense of control over yourself and will be less likely to sound or feel like you are blindly lashing out. Fourth, whenever possible use humor and focus on the positive aspects of your differences as a way of relieving tension and supporting the other person's efforts at change. Fifth, and finally, plan time for a follow-up review of the changes made so that any new problems can be dealt with in the future.

PERSONAL AFFIRMATIVE ACTION

If you are a female or a minority member, you will have some additional—or at any rate, different—kinds of adjustments to make (as well as additional opportunities and advantages). Several laws have been passed in the last fifteen years prohibiting discrimination in training, hiring, promotion, and wages on the basis of such things as sex, race, and age. The best places to look for employment if you wish to take advantage of this trend are large companies or those with federal contracts, where the laws are more strictly enforced. Look, also, at any company where an employer is personally responsive to these affirmative action guidelines.

If you are hired by a company where female or minority employees are not numerous, you need to exercise extra care in orienting yourself. Be yourself, do not go to extremes to blend in *or* to emphasize your differences. And, it is especially important to accept the existing situation, if it is essentially a fair one. Do not demand special treatment, and do not go on a crusade to change attitudes if your presence seems to be resented. Be friendly and give your co-workers time. Competition is much stiffer today for white males due to this new legislation, and it is not surprising that some of them resent it. So, if you encounter angry reactions, do not be oversensitive. Do try your best to make friends with colleagues that you like, since informal gossip and lunch times can be the best sources of important information and contacts for promotion in a large organization.

If you feel that you are being discriminated against within the organization once you settle in your job, there are several places where you may seek assistance. Unless you have a trusted lawyer or supervisor, the best source of information is the Equal Employment Opportunity Commission. Before making a complaint, be sure that you have facts and dates to back up your accusations. Keep written notes on all conversations and events that you feel demonstrate discrimination against you.

If you are a minority member, female, or older person who is hired into a situation where you are a pioneer—a tradition breaker—tread carefully. Everything that has been said applies especially to you. Be as responsible as you can, move cautiously, and listen and watch carefully for those cues discussed earlier that convey behavioral norms. Try not to be negative or defensive. By responding to your situation with care and sensitivity, you can help to open more jobs like yours to a larger segment of the population. These new changes in employer policies are a great step forward, and now is just the right time to take advantage of them, and to support this broadening of equal opportunity in our culture.

THE IDEAL JOB REVISITED

In addition to learning how to mesh smoothly with all kinds of people in the gears of an organization, the skill of successful work adjustment usually requires learning to handle some aspects of the job environment and duties.

The second major cause of job failure according to Dunphy, is "the inability to accept the job for what it is, rather than for what the new employee thought or hoped it would be." The transition from class-room to job requires time and effort. You may not immediately understand why your company does something in a certain way. What works in practice may not always coincide with what you learned in school. And, of course, your employer presented his best side in the interview, just as you did. You may find certain routine or unpleasant duties associated with your job description that you had not anticipated. Some of the problems of romanticizing a job can be avoided by looking at the world of work as realistically as possible, and by determining what you want and don't want in a job so that you can ask accurate questions about those things in a job interview.

No matter how carefully you have searched and how realistic your job choice is, you will have to face the major challenge of accepting and adjusting to a work setting that is very different from life with parents or in school. All the things we have discussed—your envi-ronment, your image and your ways of relating to others—will prob-ably need to be modified. Having an employer or supervisor over-seeing and/or evaluating your work will be a new and, at times, an anxious experience.

A 1976 survey of employers (Endicott, 1976) indicated that the 165 employers throughout the nation listed the greatest single adjustment problem of new employees as "transition from classroom learning to job experience—relating theory to practical situations." Moving on your own from taking tests, supervised lab experience, or even ap-prenticeship to doing what you have been learning about is a big step. You will be expected to correct your own mistakes, overcome job problems, and pat yourself on the back; you may not get criticism or reassurance from others as often as you did in school. In a career, unlike the classroom, you will be missed if you oversleep, take a day off, or leave early. You will be responsible, not just for understanding the theory behind a situation, but for making it work.

In learning what responsibilities are involved in your job, you may discover it calls for things you did not learn in training, and must learn on the job. A primary example of such a skill that cannot be learned from books, has already been discussed: the art of getting along with all kinds of people, including some who are very different from you, or some that you may not even like. Another skill that employers mention often is effective communication, especially in writing. Many jobs not filled by English majors nonetheless require written communication: reports, memos, minutes, newsletters, and public relations information. You will also need patience. You may not get a raise or a promotion every time you think you deserve it, and your hard work will not always be appreciated. Nor will you be able to change everything that you think should be changed. You may not have as much responsibility or voice in some matters as you would like, at least at first.

A work situation can be fun, informal, and comfortable, but it is also scheduled and structured. Your part in the organization is taken seriously by everyone. Your first job will be a world of new opportunities and new responsibilities.

CHARTING YOUR GROWTH IN AN ORGANIZATION

In Chapter 5, Gerald Cosgrave's World of Work cube was used to organize occupations according to the level of responsibility, the specific type of work performed, and the kind of enterprise in which one might be employed. Cosgrave's schema is helpful because it shows how one may apply his or her skills, interests, and values in a variety of settings. His map is much like a state road map. It gives general directions for getting from one area of the world of work to another, but it does not give us more specific details about roads and alleys within a particular work setting. To complete our overview of potential avenues for your career growth, we need a more detailed map for charting the course of your career within a particular organization.

Professor Edgar Schein of the Sloan School of Management at the Massachusetts Institute of Technology has provided us with a practical means of charting growth opportunities in organizations.[1] Schein suggests that the best way of looking at career advancement within a given organization is in terms of the cone shown in Figure 8.1.

Schein's career cone illustrates that there are three ways of growing within an organization: inwardly, vertically, and horizontally. The first form of growth, *movement toward the inner circle*, is probably the least familiar to you of the three because it is not necessarily accompanied by a visible change in position or title. Also, unlike many forms of growth, it may not require that you develop new skills to be successful at it. Your progress on this dimension will be measured

1. E. H. Schein, The Individual, the Organization, and the Career: A Conceptual Scheme. *Journal of Applied Behavioral Science*, 1971 (7) 401–426.

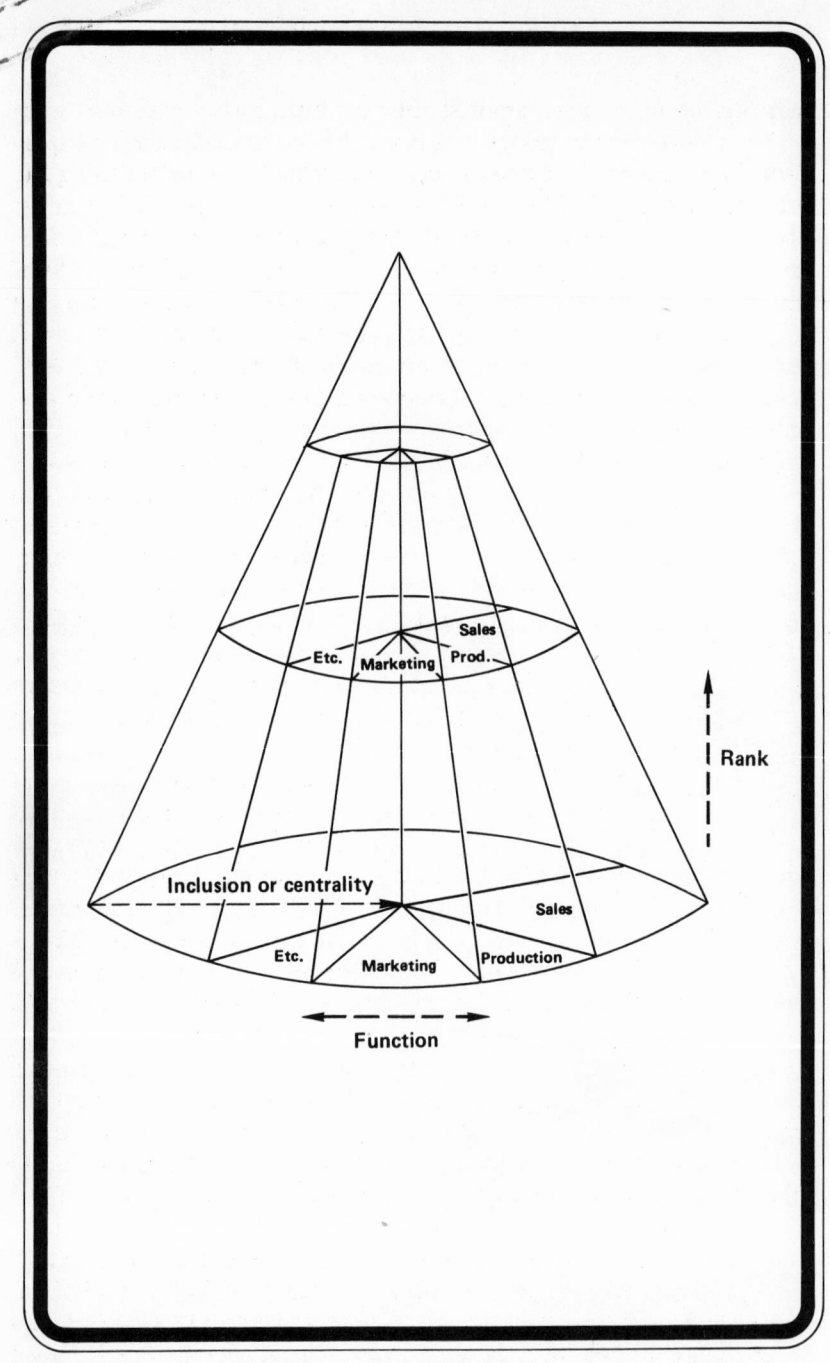

Fig. 8.1 *A three-dimensional model of an organization.* [*E. H. Schein, "The Individual, the Organization, and the Career: A Conceptual Scheme,"* Journal of Applied Behavioral Science *7(1971):401–426.*]

in terms of your interpersonal relationships, not necessarily your position. As a new employee, you will have to prove to your supervisor that you can be trusted and are dedicated to accomplishing the goals of the organization. Your first test as a new employee will occur when your supervisor passes on to you your first organizational "secret" such as the reasons why a particular decision was made or who is in with the boss and why. The sharing of this secret may be a prelude to a request for help or support from you in carrying out certain actions or decisions. If you pass the first test, others will follow. The secrets that are shared will become increasingly important and you will sense that you are becoming a more central member of the inner core of decision makers within the organization. Your status will thus be as much dependent upon who you know as what you do. Failure to pass this test of confidence may be costly in terms of being passed over for a promotion and being an outsider to information that affects your work. Passing the test, however, may not always be the only or even the best choice. If your find yourself in an organization where sharing inside information puts you in a position that is morally or ethically uncomfortable for you, this may be the signal you need to begin looking around for openings in other departments or in other organizations.

Generally speaking, the higher your position the more access you will have to privileged information within the organization. Individuals at the top of the organization need more information to make decisions that are critical to the entire organization. Thus, movement toward the inner core is often accompanied by a promotional change in title. There are, however, a number of circumstances in which a trusted employee at the lower levels of the organization may be called upon for input into key decisions because of his or her specialized knowledge or informal leadership status.

The second form of growth, vertical *movement up the organizational ranks* is probably the most familiar. Achievement by moving up the organizational ladder is a common standard for success to most Americans. We are all familiar with the story of the unskilled worker who through diligence and a willingness to acquire new skills is eventually promoted all the way to the president's chair in the organization. As a new employee, your potential for promotion within the organization will be measured in terms of both your trustworthiness and your capacity to take on increasingly greater levels of responsibility for complex tasks and for supervising others. As we discussed previously, your tolerance for stress and your willingness to continue your professional education will also play an important role in determining how successful you are at accomplishing this form of growth.

The third form of professional growth described by Schein involves a *rotation across* a series of *functions* within the organization. Rather than moving upward, you may move horizontally across positions at the same level. Many management-training programs use this form of growth as a means of exposing new employees to the different facets of an organization. As a new sales representative, for example, you may spend several weeks in the production department then be rotated across other departments until you have been exposed to the inner workings of the entire organization. This short-term approach to horizontal mobility may also be the source of long-term growth for some employees. It's not uncommon, for example, to find an employee who has worked in several departments during his or her career, all at the same level of responsibility. A highly skilled graphics designer may be assigned to different departments depending on the project that needs his or her expertise; a teacher may transfer schools in the same school district; and an insurance agent may switch from life to auto insurance sales. In each of these situations, the employee is using the same set of transferable skills to perform related functions. A special advantage of making a series of lateral moves such as these is that it may put you in touch with new learning opportunities and keep you professionally fresh. When coupled with an active refinement of your management skills, a broad range of experience can also be a valuable asset when you are seeking a promotion or a new job.

Our picture of the avenues for career development is now complete. We have a general map of the work place and a map that highlights avenues for growth within particular work settings. In the paragraphs that remain we will look at what you can do to promote more actively your career growth through the pursuit of professional development opportunities and wise decision making.

PERSONAL DEVELOPMENT

When you take a job, you have entered into a contract with your employer. In return for your contribution of labor and talent, you receive wages and certain other benefits. Be mindful of the fact that you also work for yourself, however, and one of your goals during your career should be your own development. It may be helpful to start the process by identifying interests and skills that you have which your current position does not permit you to utilize. These could be of benefit to the organization, and your supervisor might be responsive to a well-presented statement explaining why you should be permitted to add new duties to your current responsibilities. Supervisors will tell you that they spend a good deal of time checking to see that employees do their required work; the person who completes essential task assignments and asks for more is likely to be a valued employee. Projections are that a vast number of jobs will exist years from now that are not in existence today. The training that you have attained will not necessarily prepare you for jobs that will exist ten years from now. Throughout this text, however, we have emphasized the idea that education, job training, and decision making are life-long processes. Learning how to learn is an important skill, one that you should continue to use once you finish your formal education. Professional conferences, work friendships, journals, and news media are often helpful in keeping up on what's happening in your field and related fields. Many employers have plans for paying a portion of an employee's continuing education. You may find that taking some courses in areas new to you or volunteering helps you perform your current job better, as well as preparing you for a better job.

Most employers will be as interested as you are in your personal and professional growth. The company benefits by developing talent within its ranks, with an eye to present competence and future promotion. Take advantage of opportunities that come your way. Increasing your skills and knowledge is a good way to enhance your value to an employer. Managerial obsolescence, which threatens managers committed to security rather than growth, is a major problem in business. By keeping current in your field, you can avoid becoming obsolete. Being concerned with your continued development will help you maintain occupational viability and vitality.

The major ingredient in the personal and professional development of many workers is their relationship with a mentor. The mentor is often a boss or prestigious older colleague; someone you "hit it off" with who functions as a friend, teacher, and surrogate parent. This figure is a primary source of the nonacademic information and confidence which need to be developed for successful work adjustment. From him or her you can learn how to implement and apply ideas and to develop influence. The mentor relationship is usually personal enough so that the new worker can request feedback, ask questions about other people, air misgivings, and get honest advice about how to best use the employment situation for personal development. The mentor also functions as a role model. By watching the way she or he deals with many situations, you can refine the use of all five career skills.

Female and minority employees may have more difficulty in attracting a mentor, or in keeping the relationship running smoothly. This may happen because such persons are not totally welcome in a particular work setting, or because they seem different and old timers are a bit afraid of them. Since so many potential mentors are men, there are also some additional complications for females: beliefs held by many men about what behaviors are appropriate for women, teasing or gossip about the relationship, and the possibility of sexual attraction. There are no rules for handling these pitfalls effectively. Sensitivity to the mentor and to the work environment is called for. Although a mentor must essentially be a volunteer, you can invite the support of a potential mentor by asking questions or showing an interest in how that person's job is done. As with any other situation in a new work environment, patience and quiet observation are best at first.

The skill of maintaining a successful career adjustment, it should now be clear, is composed of the abilities needed to adapt and to grow along with shifts in the environment and changes in oneself. These include the capabilities for social interaction, communication, and for continued learning, as well as the regular use of the first four skills learned in this text. Keeping abreast of satisfaction and fit in any job requires that we regularly reassess our feelings, values, beliefs, goals, interest, skills, and experience—all of which accumulate and change over the years. We must also be sensitive to the job market and the economy, to changing requirements and possibilities of other jobs and new opportunities. Organizing this stream of new information within the structure of our decision skills should help us to know when and how we wish to act to reach our evolving career goals.

PROMOTIONAL STRATEGIES

Your attention to your own personal development and growth will inevitably lead to expanded interests and abilities and a desire for new challenges. Depending upon your development as an individual and the direction your company is taking, this need for change can be met in a variety of ways. As we have discussed previously, these include a move to another organization or another career area, a move up in your company's hierarchy, a lateral move to another area or department, or even just a move toward greater inclusion in decision-making processes that affect you (illustrated by Schein's organizational cone). This can be as simple as asking to be included in policy-making or managerial meetings or as complex as a planned campaign to be qualified and considered for a certain promotion or job.

Whether you enter a job with the general goal of being promoted or are aiming for advancement into a specific position, there are professional and interpersonal hints and strategies that will help you to move along your planned path and to meet transitions and obstacles more smoothly. First, begin early in your job to document your successes. When you offer good ideas, institute new policies or contribute to the solution of a problem, put it in a written report as a memo or get it into the minutes of a meeting. Make sure the people who do the promoting get a copy, and keep a copy for yourself. Save letters of recommendation. If someone you trust commends or thanks you for a job well done, you may want to ask them to put it in writing and/or make sure your superiors hear the news. Second, be sure that you fully understand the requirements and demands of your target position and are willing and able to meet them. Third, work on building a system of formal and informal connections. Make an effort to cooperate with your supervisor and understand his or her problems. Do the same with others in higher positions who may be influential in choosing people to promote. Keep in touch with friends you make in other areas and departments and in other companies. Besides enjoying their company, you may find that their shop talk and problems can provide valuable information about what to expect and about where job openings may occur. In the case of friends or mentors that you trust, let them know how things are going for you and what your future plans are so that they can put in a good word for you if the opportunity arises. (You may be able to do the same for them.) Your immediate supervisor may be a good person to confide in, but not always. If you are uncomfortable about your relationship, if someone else is really making the decisions, or if you are after his or her job, he or she may not be the best person to choose as an ally. If you don't get along with your supervisor and feel he or she will block your chances for advancement, you may want to plan for a lateral move to another area where the environment is more favorable. Finally, when you have made a decision to try for a specific position or to make a move within a specific time frame, share this with your support group and suggest things you have thought of that they might do to help. Whenever it seems appropriate, share your goals with the people who will make the promotion or do the hiring. Present to them your documentation of your work successes, your reasons for being interested in the change, and your beliefs about what you will have to offer in the new position.

CAREER EXPANSION: MOVING UP, ACROSS, OR OUT

No job or living environment is ideal, they all have their peculiarities and problems. Even the job that approaches the ideal will be dissatisfying some of the time. Discomfort can be an important prelude to growth, but how do you know when it is time to look for a different position? To move up, across, or out? How frustrated, bored, or disappointed must you be before you say, "Enough is enough" and begin the process of change? These are difficult questions to deal with; there are no pat answers or formulas, only those that you find in yourself. There are, however, some areas to explore and questions to ask as you sort through your motivation to change.

Start with yourself, where the growth cycle begins and ends. Do you want more money, more (or less) responsibility, a new set of tasks, a different life-style? Have your career goals changed since you started at your job? How do they differ if they have changed? Are you a victim of the Peter Principle? And, last but very important, how much of your dissatisfaction is due to your attitudes and behaviors, which will follow you to any job you choose? Next, look to the organization. Does it ask too much or give too little, leaving you with the feeling of being burnt out and unappreciated? Does the job have a negative effect on the other aspects of your life-style, your social involvements, and your leisure pursuits? Has your employer made comments about your work performance falling off, indicating that he or she also sees that you are less involved in your work than before? Is the employer supportive of your need for change or is such change viewed as a threat to the status quo? Is there an unresolved conflict at work that haunts you from day-to-day? After you have explored these questions, look at the options you will have if you stay where you are. Can you redefine your position (sometimes even the slightest alteration can make a big difference) or move to another one within the firm to save the benefits you have accumulated?

Lastly, look to the benefits of moving out. Where do you want to live? What work will you be doing there? Before we further discuss the process of changing jobs, however, let us look at the whole idea of job change. Years ago employers tended to view with some concern the employee who had a vocational history marked by several jobs; people tended to remain with the organization where they began work, moving up or across rather than out. While this is still often the case, today's American work force is more job mobile than ever before. Every year ten per cent of the labor force changes jobs. The average American can expect to change jobs at least three or four times during the course of his or her career. The prospective employee who has a good explanation for job movement can usually locate a new position. If your record as an employee is marked by frequent or directionless moves, however, you could experience difficulty in looking for still another job. Informed decisions made in the early stages of your job search can help to keep you out of a job you may want to leave in six months. Consider the advantages and disadvantages of available jobs. Be realistic about your strengths and limitations when you assess the requirements of new jobs. On the basis of adequate information, make a decision about what you would like to do and how you are going to do it. If possible, stay in your present position while conducting your job search. An employer is more likely to hire someone who already has a job. (The "interviewing for information" approach is a useful way of searching out new prospects while maintaining control over your present job situation. So is taking on some job responsibilities that involve meeting the public or other people in your field.)

Regardless of what you do, your overriding goal should be to retain a balanced perspective on where you are, what you want to do, and how you will go about getting what you want. This requires that you be thorough and clearcut in your approach to building your future. By doing so, you can increase the odds of saying to yourself in the future, "I have lived the way I wanted. I have enjoyed my career."

PROMOTING CONSTRUCTIVE CHANGE

Imagine yourself in the following situations:

1. During an employment interview, the recruiter has asked you a question or made a comment that leads you to believe you are being discriminated against or are being judged on the basis of your gender or social group status. How will you handle this situation?

2. You are a new employee. Your colleagues have implied to you that you are being given preferential treatment because of your gender, race, or social group membership. You'd like to change their attitudes because you don't think you are being judged fairly.

3. Your supervisor is making heavy demands on your time. You haven't been able to meet those demands without putting in a considerable amount of overtime. The pressure of the job has been causing you to cut back on leisure and social pursuits that

have been important to you. It doesn't look as though the situation will change in the near future.

4. You have a strong but unexpressed difference of opinion with a colleague about the way a project should be done. You've been holding back your opinion for several weeks and it's beginning to distress you.

5. After a year on the job, you did not receive the raise you had hoped for. You believe you deserve a raise and want to take steps to get it.

6. Your recent request for a promotion was denied, but you don't know why.

7. You've been doing the same job for five years and have been feeling bored and restless recently. You don't know why your feelings have changed but you are becoming more and more distressed about your situation.

8. You are a departmental supervisor. Two of your employees have had a considerable amount of conflict recently. You'd like to change this situation as soon as you can because it's beginning to affect the general morale of your staff.

9. You're going to retire in two years. How will you prepare for the change?

Pick two of the situations described above and apply them to your own career in the future. For each situation, try to identify its potential causes and outline a strategy for resolving or changing it. Use the procedure outlined below in developing your change strategy.

1. What are the causes of this situation?

2. What is the worst possible way I can handle this problem?
   a. How would I behave if I were to use a strategy of *irrational approach* to changing the situation?
   b. How would I behave if I were to use an *irrational avoidance* strategy?

3. To change this situation to make it more constructive I would have to alter my behaviors in the following ways. Identify specific behaviors that you would need to change.

   a. _____

   b. _____

   c. _____

   d. _____

4. To change this situation to make it more positive or constructive, others would have to change their behaviors in the following ways. Identify the specific behaviors that they would have to change.

    a. _____

    b. _____

    c. _____

    d. _____

5. How will you communicate your desire to change the situation to others?

6. How much responsibility will you take for promoting the change? How much responsibility will you share with others?

7. Using the information from the questions above, outline the specific steps you will take to create this change.

    a. _____

    b. _____

    c. _____

    d. _____

    e. _____

REFERENCES

Dunphy, P.W. *Career Development for the College Student.* Cranston, Rhode Island: The Carroll Press, 1973.

Endicott, F.S. Report of the Thirty-first Annual Survey of Policy and Practice in the Employment of College and University Graduates in Business and Industry. Evanston, Ill.: Placement Office, Northeastern University, 1976.

Qualities Employers Like, Dislike in Job Applications. *Final Report of Statewide Employer Survey.* Austin, Texas. The Advisory Council for Technical–Vocational Education in Texas, 1975.

Appendix A

Experiential Exercises

Personal Coat of Arms
Guidelines for the Personal Journal
Decision-Making Vignettes
Instructions for the Lifeline Activity
Explorations in Life-style Choice
Guidelines for the Occupational Report
You, The Employer
Practice Job Interviews

181

PERSONAL COAT OF ARMS[1]

In years gone by, families created personal coats of arms to present themselves to others. Their coats of arms often expressed a bit of their family's history and beliefs and activities that were important to them. The activity will allow you to act something like our ancestors. It invites you to create your own coat of arms and to introduce yourself to others in your class through your creation.

On page 183 you will find a coat of arms, divided into six sections. In each section, make a drawing to express your thoughts in response to the directions. Do not use words except in section six. Your drawings can be simple, as they express your feelings.

1. In section one, express in a drawing your own greatest personal accomplishment.

2. In section two, express in a drawing your family's greatest accomplishment.

3. In section three, express in a drawing one or two things that people who care about you have suggested you do for a living.

4. In section four, express in a drawing the thing you like most about being a student.

5. In section five—if you had the time, money, and opportunity— show in a drawing what occupation you would ideally want to enter.

6. In section six, list the things you want most from work.

---

1. Adapted from Simon, S. B., Hawley, R. C., and Britton, D. D., *Composition for Personal Growth: Values Clarification Through Writing.* Copyright © 1973 by Hart Publishing Company. Reprinted by permission.

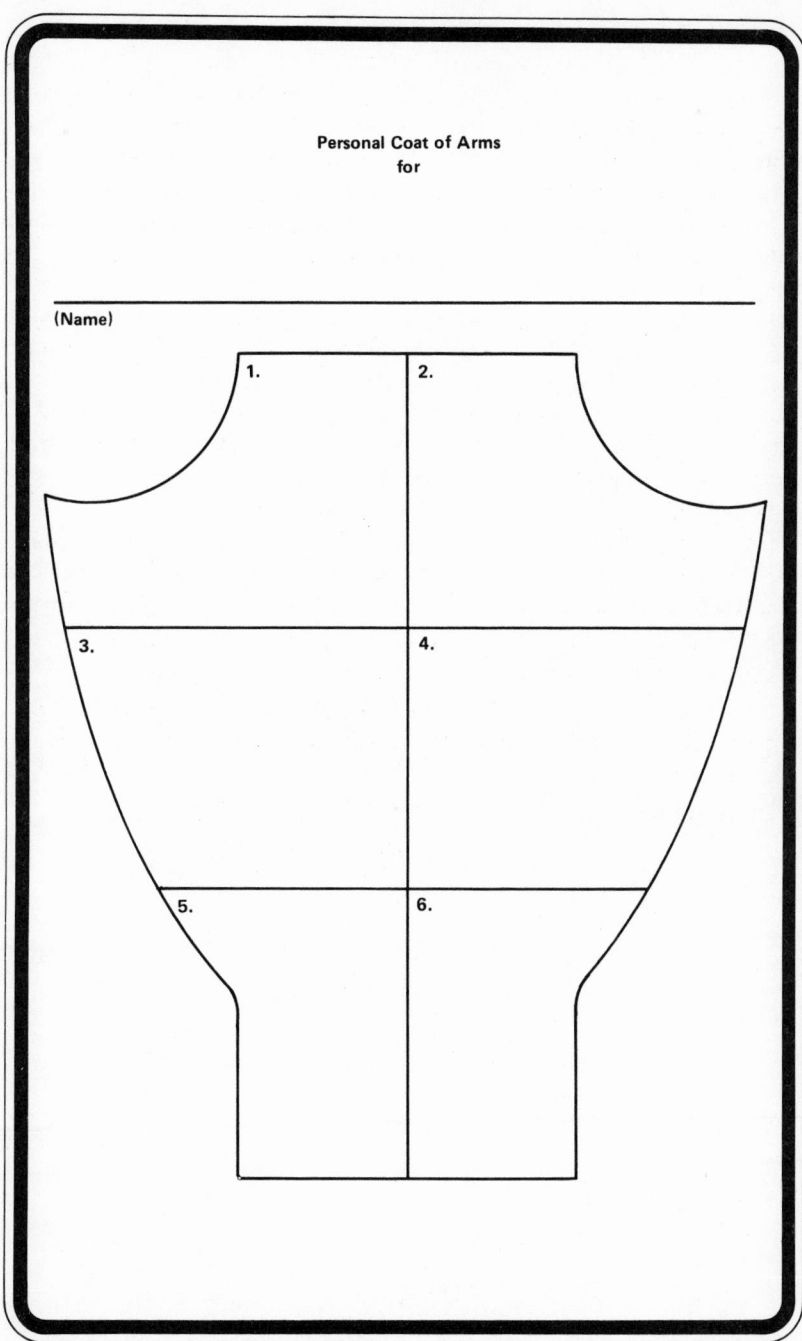

Figure A1   Personal Coat of Arms.

GUIDELINES FOR THE PERSONAL JOURNAL

The personal journal is a diary designed to help you become more aware of yourself in the career planning process and to help you integrate your experiences inside and outside of the classroom.

Your journals should consist of two entries. The first entry, *What I did*, may cover a variety of activities such as your reactions to class sessions, observations of and conversations with others about your work, ideas about your interests, abilities, and values, volunteer or work activities that you are pursuing, and conversations you have had with others about their career goals.

The second entry, *How I reacted to what I did and what it means to me*, should focus on the thoughts and feelings the activity stimulated in you. It should also tell what these reactions mean to you as you think about yourself in the process of exploring and defining a career objective.

Your entries need not be lengthy, but each entry should be made shortly after the activity has occurred. Each entry should reflect an attempt to integrate what you have experienced with your current thoughts about selecting a career.

Your journals may be collected at different points throughout the seminar so that comments can be made by your instructor to assist you in the process of self- and occupational exploration.

On page 185 there is a sample page of a journal for you to copy into a notebook. Make a journal page (or as many as are needed) for each week and fill it out as discussed here. At the end of the term copy the "Personal Journal Summary Self-Review" from page 185 into your notebook and fill it out.

_____

Name

_____

Date

Personal Journal Entries for Week

What I did or what happened	How I reacted

_____
Name

_____
Date

_____
Personal Journal Summary Self-Review
(What I have learned about myself and my career plans this term.)

DECISION–MAKING VIGNETTES

Mark Manycredits

Mark Manycredits has reached the point where he must declare a major, and he is having great difficulty making a decision. His real dream is to go to law school. His high school grade average was a 3.4, and his college grades are about the same. On interest tests he scores very high on law, and he loves debating and public speaking. But he is afraid he might not be able to reach his goal in the field of law. His father says he will have trouble in law school admissions and in hiring; that he will have to do better than others to prove himself because he is black. His college advisor tells him the field of law is overcrowded anyway. If he tries and fails to get into law school, he will have a B.A. in political science, which won't really qualify him for any specific job.

Mark is also very interested in the possibility of being a medical technician, and feels this might be a less risky option. He has a cousin who is a lab technician and he helped her one summer while doing volunteer work at the hospital where she works. She is well paid and has plenty of autonomy on the job. Mark's family feels this second option is more realistic for him. They are struggling financially to help put Mark through college, and they don't want him to risk wasting those four years.

What should Mark do to resolve his problem in a planful way?

Helen and Harry Household

Helen and Harry Household have been married seven years. She is 30 and he is 32. They have two children, ages four and six. Helen made good grades in high school and enjoyed studying. She got a scholarship to her hometown college, but dropped out after two years because she was undecided about her major. She took a secretarial job (which she didn't really like) and soon afterward she met and married Harry. He has a B.A. in accounting and is just beginning to work his way up in a large firm. Helen has enjoyed doing volunteer work and being home with the kids, but now she feels ready to go back to school. She is anxious to get started soon, because she feels she is getting older, and because she has discovered several kinds of jobs she thinks she might like. Helen feels they could afford to put their four-year-old in a preschool if they scrimped a little, or that she could go to evening classes while Harry babysits. She would prefer to go daytimes so she could spend evenings with the family.

Harry wants her to wait until the children are older and he is making more money, before she goes back to school. He's just beginning to enjoy having a little extra money for luxuries. He suggested that if she is bored at home she could look for another secretarial job for a few years. That way Helen could get out of the house and bring in a little money instead of spendiing it.

What should Helen and Harry do to resolve their problem in a planful way?

Molly Mathwhiz

Molly Mathwhiz has wanted to work with computers ever since she first saw one at a high school science fair. She can't decide whether to go away to a university and get a B.A. in computer science, or to go to the two-year program at the technical college in her hometown. Molly's high school grade average is 2.9, with her math grades being much higher. Both schools she is considering have good programs in various computer areas, but her father wants very much for her to have a college degree. Her dad believes that having a B.A. will help her get a better paying and more prestigious job, and that people will look up to her more if she has a college degree. Her high school boyfriend has a good job in their hometown, and wants her to go to tech, rather than away to college, so that they can get married and "settle down."

Molly has some savings, but she will have to work no matter where she goes to school. She can probably get along on less money at tech since she can live at home. Molly would like to please both her father and her boyfriend, but the most important thing to her is to decide which degree would provide a better background and lead to more exciting job offers. She isn't sure she wants to get married right away, but everyone assumes they are engaged, and she's afraid if she goes away to school he might meet someone else.

What should Molly do to resolve her dilemma in a planful way?

INSTRUCTIONS FOR THE LIFELINE ACTIVITY

We each hope to shape a well-rounded, realistic future. But before we can anticipate the future, we need to explore what has happened in the past and how we are in the present. To do so, we are going to use a line drawn across a blank sheet of paper to plot our development as persons to date, and to project our development in the future.

Borrowing from the recollections you had about yourself in the past, draw a line across the sheet of paper starting with your birth in the lower left hand corner and extend it to the present. Be sure to leave space for the future as we will be coming to that in a little while. In drawing your line, feel free to put in peaks and valleys. Peaks and valleys can be used to show major events that have affected your life such as moving from one place to another, changing school, friends, births and deaths in your family, and jobs you have had. They can be used to describe your feelings at different points in your life.

Be sure to indicate "marker" events in your life—turning points where decisions were made by yourself or others—and how they changed your life. Mark these with an "X."

Star the high points in your life to date and put a minus sign on the low points.

After you have completed the line from past to present, extend yourself into the future and project what you expect the future will hold using a dotted line. Indicate the kinds of events that you anticipate having to deal with in the future—and how they will shape your lifeline.

EXPLORATIONS IN LIFE-STYLE CHOICE

This set of exercises will help you gain a clearer idea of how you currently integrate your daily activities into your overall life-style and the needs you are meeting with them.

The activities that follow provide you with an opportunity to become aware of how you spend your time, the activities that you value, and how, in making decisions about time, you are expressing some of your personal needs and beliefs. This knowledge will help you get a clearer perspective on your current life situation and how it relates to your career goals.

Exercise No. 1: Energy Giving and Energy Getting Activities

During a typical day, you no doubt have noticed that certain types of activities serve to restore your energy, refresh your mind, and relax you, while other activities seem to deplete your energy, exhaust you, and tire you out. In other words, the energy flow for any activity will be positive or negative. Take several sheets of paper and generate a list within the group of activities that fit the following criteria: (Write each of the following on separate pieces of paper.)

Energy Flow Rating Scale

+ + = Activities that for me are very relaxing, refreshing, enjoyable

+ = Activities that for me are somewhat relaxing, refreshing, enjoyable

0 = Activities that for me are neither relaxing nor tiring, just "neutral"

− = Activities that for me are somewhat mentally tiring or exhausting

− − = Activities that for me are very tiring and exhausting

The rule of thumb that you should use in generating this list is that you want to create as broad a list in as short a time as possible. To do so you will not examine each activity as you record it, but will simply throw ideas out to make sure all possibilities are covered. Once you have exhausted all of your ideas, you can go back and review them and eliminate or combine some of them.

The next task is for you to apply the items to yourself during a typical week. Look at the list of activities you have generated and identify activities that best exemplify a typical week for you. Feel free to add items if you wish to make your list more representative for you personally. Turn to Fig. A2 and record each activity you have listed over the appropriate energy flow category, + + to − −. By doing so, you will gain a clearer perspective on the balance of a typical week in your life.

Once you have completed your list, ask yourself the following questions:

1. Is my typical week balanced the way I would like it to be?
2. Do I typically expend more energy than I receive? If so, how does it affect my general outlook toward life?
3. Am I spending more time in pleasurable activities to the neglect of some important energy–spending tasks?
4. Do I build in rewards (energy–giving activities) after working hard at certain tasks?
5. If I wanted to alter the way I spend my time, what things would I give up or add on? Will I do it? Starting when?

Exercise No. 2: My Time Is My Life-Style

The first experiment was designed to help you get a feel for how your energies flow in your interactions with your environments. This

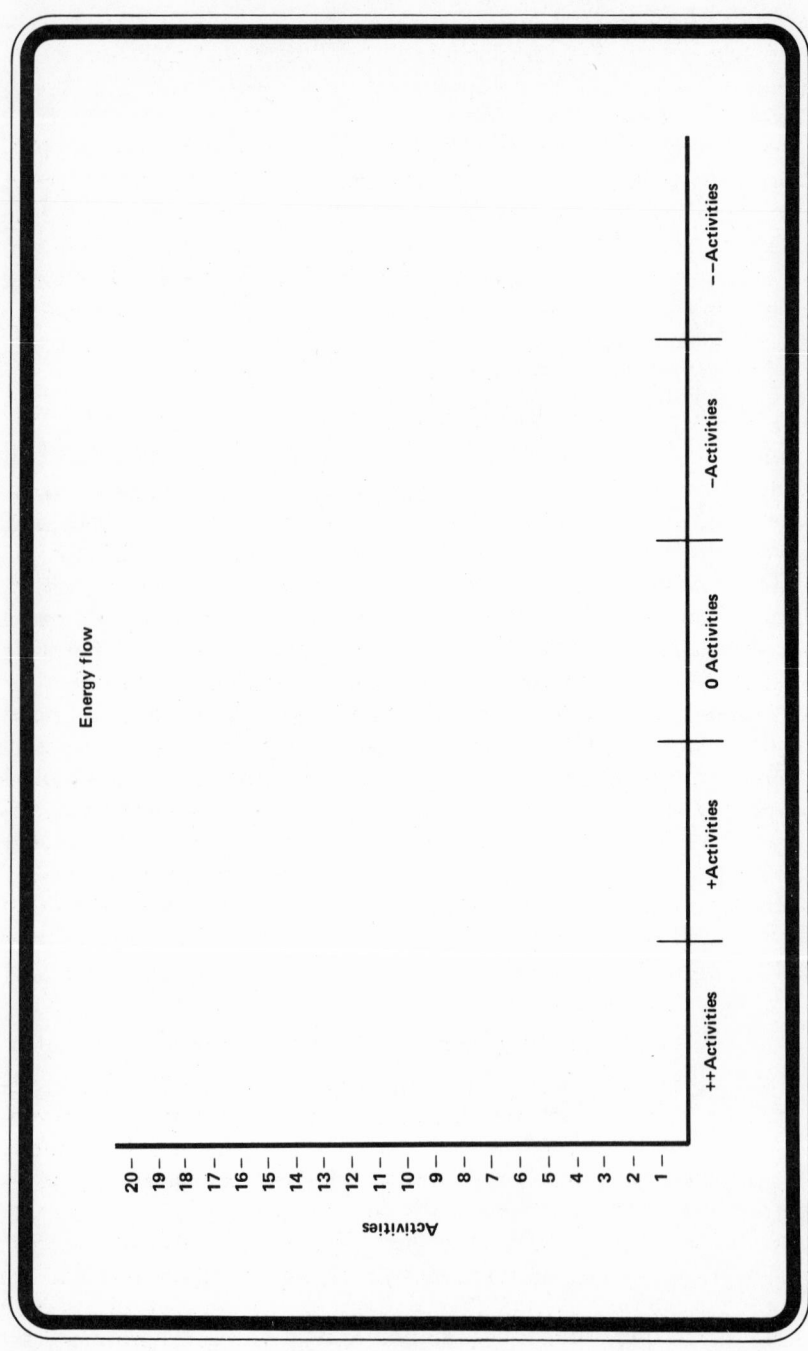

Figure A2   Energy flow chart.

activity is designed to help you get a clearer picture of your current life-style; that is the proportion of time spent in study–work, leisure–recreation, and kinship–friendship activities during a typical week.

To complete this activity, all you need to do is record the activities that apply to you during a typical week at college and write them in the appropriate area on Fig. A3. As before, you will need to draw the diagram in Fig. A3 on a piece of paper. At the end of the week, review what you have recorded and ask yourself the following questions:

1. Is this a typical week for me?
2. Is this the way I want to live in the future? If not, what would I change about my life-style? How would I make those changes? When?

Again, discussion should be focused on helping you more clearly view your current life-style and how you might wish to alter the way you live as you plan toward the future. To engage you more completely in the process of comparing the present with your future "ideal" life-style, you may wish to draw two life-style triangles on a sheet of paper. Using data from the life-style grid you have just completed, first draw a triangle that represents the shape of your lifestyle now—that is, so many units of leisure-recreation on one side, so many units of study-work on the second side, and so many units of kinship-friendship on the third side. After you complete this triangle, draw a second one that represents your ideal life-style, the one you want to shape through the choices you are making now. Compare the triangles and focus on how you can make the present more comfortable, and on what you can do starting now to build toward your future ideal.

Exercise No. 3: **Life Needs and Life-Style Choices**

As you noted in the companion reading, "Variations on a Lifestyle Theme," Abraham Maslow suggested that each of our daily activities can meet one or several needs. Work, for example, provides money to purchase food and drink, to obtain shelter and security, and gives us opportunities to experience a sense of belonging, esteem, and self-realization. By reviewing how you spent your time over a typical week, you can begin to identify more clearly the needs that you are currently meeting in your life. In doing so, you may find that you will want to reprioritize some of your activities to meet some important needs that you are not presently meeting.

192

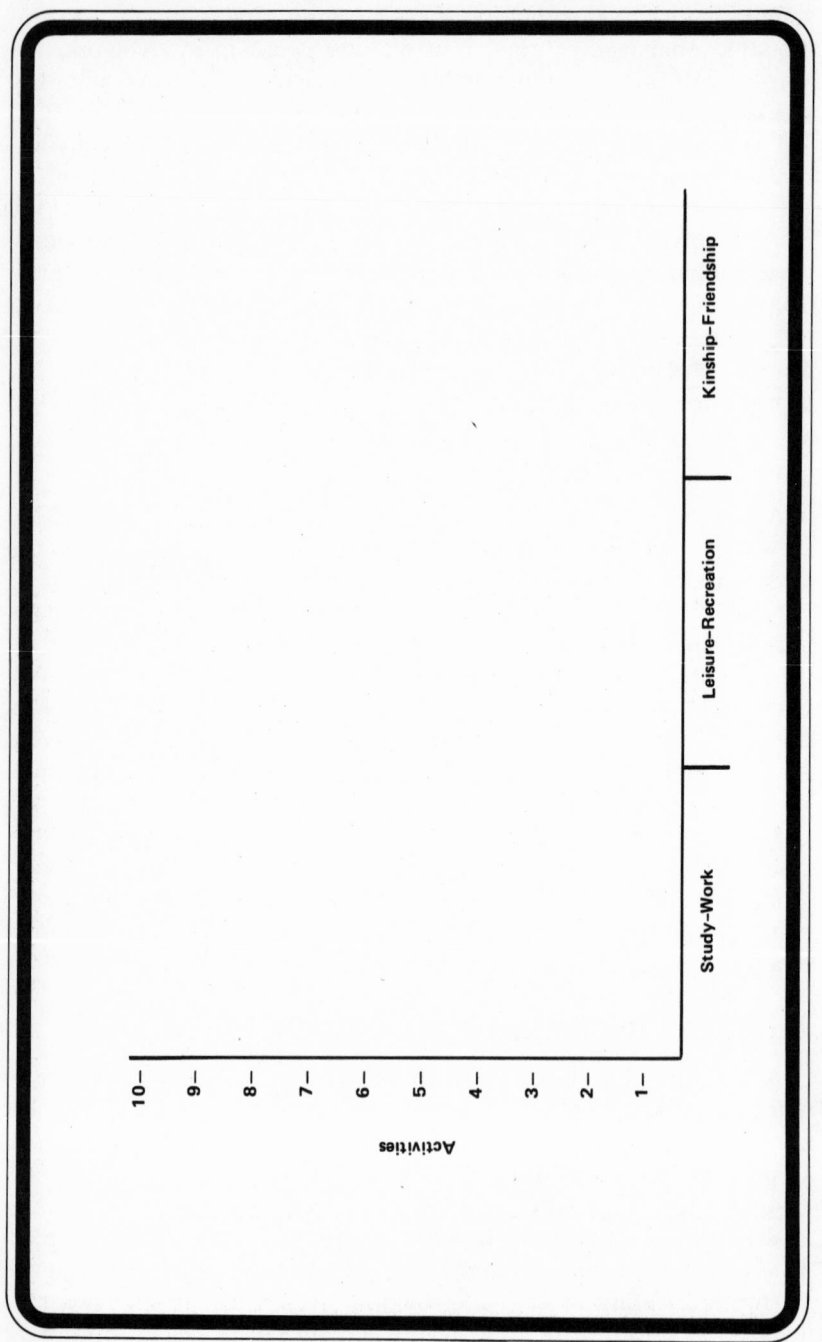

Figure A3   Current life-styles.

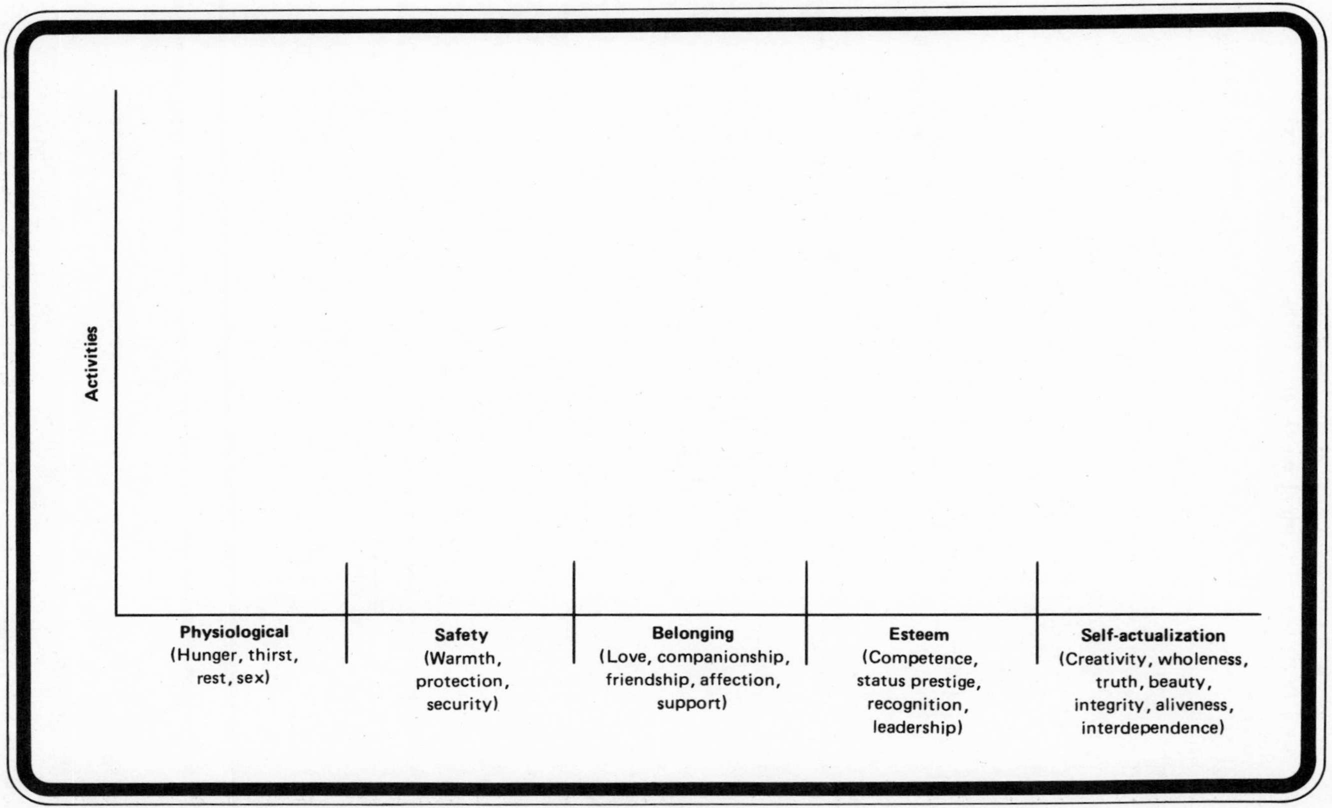

Activities

Physiological
(Hunger, thirst, rest, sex)

Safety
(Warmth, protection, security)

Belonging
(Love, companionship, friendship, affection, support)

Esteem
(Competence, status prestige, recognition, leadership)

Self-actualization
(Creativity, wholeness, truth, beauty, integrity, aliveness, interdependence)

Figure A4 Life needs and life-style choices.

To complete this exercise, copy Fig. A4 and list the activities you engaged in during a typical week above the needs they appear to be meeting.

In reviewing the patterns of the needs that you have met during a typical week, you may experience a desire to meet specific needs more frequently. Use another sheet of paper to identify these needs and plan strategies for increasing your likelihood of meeting them.

Divide the paper into two columns; one labeled "Needs I would like to meet more often," the other, "Activities that will help me meet them."

Needs I would like to meet more often	Activities that will help me meet them
1. _____	A _____
_____	B _____
	C _____
2. _____	A _____
_____	B _____
	C _____
3. _____	A _____
_____	B _____
	C _____
4. _____	A _____
_____	B _____
	C _____

GUIDELINES FOR THE *OCCUPATIONAL REPORT*

The *Occupational Report* will help you pull together and compare information you have generated about yourself with information you gather about an occupation or occupations that interest you.

Your description of your "ideal job" is the first important aspect of the *Occupational Report*. It helped you characterize your preferred life-style. The second step, the P.L.A.C.E. occupational rating activity, will allow you to compare a specific occupation or several occupations with these ideal requirements. The *Occupational Report* will allow you to summarize this information in a narrative form and project yourself into the future in the occupation that currently has most appeal to you.

Plan on covering five steps in preparing your *Occupational Report:*

1. Select an occupation from the P.L.A.C.E. activity that you would like to describe in depth.

2. Identify the resources you have used in exploring that occupation, including conversations you have had with others in the field (one instructor and one worker are required), places you have visited or done volunteer work in, and written materials you have read.

3. Compare the information you have obtained with the requirements of your ideal job. Indicate in what ways and how frequently the occupation would allow you to exercise your ideals. Also indicate the skills you would need to be successful in this occupation and how you would go about acquiring them.

4. Identify and briefly describe occupations that are related to the one you explored. Indicate which ones you would consider as alternatives to your primary occupation.

5. Pretend you have the ability to see the future clearly. Based upon what you know about yourself now, the occupation you explored in your occupational report, and what you have learned about how individuals continue to develop over their adult years, write four "notes to yourself" in the future. The notes should portray what is important to you and the choices you will be making at the following points in time:

    a. the remainder of this year
    b. shortly after college graduation
    c. ten years from now
    d. at retirement

YOU, THE EMPLOYER

Imagine yourself as a personnel director who is looking for a graduate of your college in his/her firm. If you are like most employers, you'll develop a rating scale of some type that lists the qualities you will be looking for in the applicants. Although each worker quality is important, you will probably decide that some will have more weight in your decision than others.

Listed below are some of the reasons employers typically mention that they use for rejecting job applicants. As an employer, your task is to rank order them from most to least important to you. Use "1" to indicate "most important" and "13" to indicate the "least important" worker characteristic for you.

After you have done this, you will compare your rankings with those of others in the group and develop a group consensus ranking. Your instructor will compare your groups' rankings with those of actual employers.

Rank	*Quality*
a. _____	Inability to get along with people, little self-confidence, and leadership potential.
b. _____	Poor academic achievement, poor grades.
c. _____	Lack of well thought out personal and career goals.
d. _____	No interest in the type of work my company performs.
e. _____	Lack of personal initiative, enthusiasm, drive.
f. _____	Inability to express oneself orally and in writing.
g. _____	Unrealistic salary demands, not willing to work up from the bottom.
h. _____	Poor personal appearance.
i. _____	Lack of involvement in extracurricular activities.
j. _____	No awareness of what my company is all about, has not read literature about it.
k. _____	Not willing to travel or move.
l. _____	Excessive interest in security and benefits rather than interest in job.
m. _____	Inadequate preparation for the position one is applying for.

PRACTICE JOB INTERVIEWS

The objective of this role-play activity is to give you the feel of an interview experience as well as objective feedback about how you behave in such a situation.

During the activity you will work with two of your classmates and each of you will play three different roles: job applicant, employer, and interview observer. As the applicant, you will brief the interviewer on what type of job you want to be interviewed for. The interviewer will ask a series of questions about your qualifications and goals. The observer will complete the rating sheet shown on page 198 and pay attention to what your job goals are and what kind of impression you make during the interview. Your instructor will tell you when to start the interviews and when to change roles.

Rating Sheet for Observers of Practice Interviews

1. Did the person establish good eye contact?

1	2	3	4	5

Looked away,   Looked directly
down at the floor   at other person

2. What was the general body posture?

1	2	3	4	5

Leaning away,   Leaning forward,
slumped   erect

3. How were hand gestures used?

1	2	3	4	5

Nervous, tense   Emphatic, strong
movements   gestures

4. What were the facial expressions?

1	2	3	4	5

Smiling, laughing,   Calm serious
nervous   expression

5. How did the person's voice sound?

1	2	3	4	5

Whispered, monotone,   Strong, clear
quivering   tone

6. At what pace did the person respond?

1	2	3	4	5

Hesitated, long   Immediate, concise
pauses, use of "uh"   response

Appendix

B

Interest and Ability Self-Assessment Activities

Interests
Functional Skills
Summary Profile

People seeking assistance in planning their careers frequently say, "I'm uncertain about which major or occupation to pursue. Is there a test that can tell me what I should do with the rest of my life?" Their question reflects a common but incomplete belief about the career planning process. While it is true that a number of students have had their tentative educational and occupational goals confirmed by tests, there are many who have found that tests opened up new areas to explore rather than defining a single choice for them. Thus, tests can be used to narrow or expand one's career options. Although we know that they may be helpful in these ways, it is also important to realize their limitations.

Just as hammers don't make good wrenches, tests don't provide useful aids to career planning when they are misused. Since tests sample around 10% of the 20,000 occupations that exist in our society, they provide only a limited view of a person's occupational possibilities. Also, because most are heavily biased toward a person's past experiences, they can reinforce stereotypic notions about which fields men and women and minorities should enter. For example, the woman who is thinking about entering a field traditionally dominated by men, such as engineering, will find her expertise as a secretary confirmed by the test but will not learn much about her potential as an engineer. The most beneficial use of a test in this situation would be to help her identify the interests and skills she will need to develop in order to become an engineer. It may involve some work on her part to pursue her new goal, but at least she'll have some suggestions on how to get there.

Another problem with tests is in the way they are scored and interpreted. We remember most those experiences in which we have been actively involved; the poem that we spent hours memorizing in grammer school; the recognition we earned for a job well done. In most occupational testing situations we are active only as long as we are taking the test. Computers and technicians score the results and counselors interpret them for us. Because the expertise for scoring and interpreting the tests rests in someone else's hands, it's easy to feel mystified by the test. We may then passively absorb the results instead of gaining a better understanding of how we have developed our abilities and interests. Small wonder that researchers have found that most people forget the results of testing shortly afterward!

In sharing these points with you, our goal is not to turn you off to tests. Instead, we want to help you recognize the limitations inherent in testing and to use the results wisely. It may be helpful to you to know that there are other, less complicated, ways of assessing your personal qualities besides taking standardized tests. One type of exploration involves examining the themes in your fantasies and aspirations, and seeing how they match the requirements of different occupations. Similarly, you can make lists of activities that you enjoy and do well, and look for commonalities among them that can be translated into work activities. You can also use self-scored inventories that tap into your interests, values, and abilities. The self-scored inventory that follows will provide you with such an opportunity to review your work interests and functional skills within John Holland's worker typology. The results of these surveys can be used to generate educational and occupational areas for exploration that are consistent with your particular work personality.

INTERESTS

As we discussed in Chapter 3, "The Emerging Self: Birth to Adolescence," John Holland believes that our interests and skills tend to group together around six common personality types:

1. *Realistic* people like to work with their hands, are often athletic, and tend to enjoy working outdoors with animals, machines, or nature.
2. *Investigative* people enjoy scientific types of activities where they engage in research to test out ideas or to develop new products.
3. *Artistic* individuals find that they most enjoy expressing ideas and feelings through writing stories and poems, painting, photography, sculpturing, and physical movement.
4. *Social* people find satisfaction in teaching, counseling, assisting and informing others.
5. *Enterprising* workers like to persuade, supervise, or lead others toward common goals, or to sell an idea or product.
6. *Conventional* persons most like activities that allow them to organize data, attend to detail, and check results for accuracy.

The purpose of this activity is to allow you to compare your current interests with each of these six types of worker personality.

On the pages that follow, you will find a number of study and work activities that will have varying degrees of appeal to you. You can indicate how much you enjoy or are interested in each activity by circling a 3, 2, 1, or 0 next to each item.

Circle "3" if you have a definite or strong interest
in the activity
For example: Making jewelry 0 1 2 (3)
Circle "2" if you have a moderate amount of interest
in the activity
For example: Selling insurance 0 1 (2) 3
Circle "1" if you have little interest in the activity
For example: Installing vending machines 0 (1) 2 3
Circle "0" if the activity has no appeal to you at all
For example: Running an addressograph
machine .... (0) 1 2 3

Do not be concerned about whether or not you have the skills to perform a particular activity; you will review your competencies in the second part of this set of surveys. Since your first reactions will produce the most reliable index of your interests, work rapidly and respond spontaneously to each item. Be sure to circle a number beside each item before moving on to the next item. Complete the entire inventory before you total your scores. That way your responses will be fresh and not delayed by having to work on calculating totals.

My Realistic (R) Interests are in . . .

1. Routing aircraft, ships, trucks, or buses .... (0) 1 2 3

2. Installing, maintaining, and repairing computers or other computer machines .... (0) 1 2 3

*3. Breeding pedigreed dogs, thoroughbred horses, or other animals .... (0) 1 2 3

4. Landscaping yards and parks 0 1 (2) 3

5. Farming the ocean for fish and other sea products.................................. (0) 1 2 3

6. Building or repairing furniture 0 1 (2) 3

7. Refining and demonstrating my athletic skills ... 0 1 2 (3)

*8. Enforcing laws to protect life and property 0 (1) 2 3

9. Creating blueprints for buildings, machines, or electrical equipment .... (0) 1 2 3

10. Guarding the safety and feeding of wildlife 0 1 (2) 3

11. Building houses or other structures 0 (1) 2 3

12. Operating emergency, rescue, or firefighting equipment .... (0) 1 2 3

13. Driving a truck, tractor, or bus .... (0) 1 2 3

14. Building or operating radio or TV equipment ... (0) 1 2 3

"0"   ☐ 0

                                                         +

Sum of circled "1's"   ☐

                                                         +

Sum of circled "2's"   ☐

                                                         +

Sum of circled "3's"   ☐

                                                         =

Grand total of circled "1's," "2's," "3's"   ☐

My Investigative (I) Interests are in . . .

1. Investigating the occupations, style of living, or
    behavior of others 0   1   2 ③

*2. Experimenting with living plants or animals to
    explore the laws of growth or heredity .... ⓪ 1   2   3

3. Designing new forms of transportation or
    communication .... ⓪ 1   2   3

4. Designing experiments to create or to test new
    drugs, chemicals, or diets .... ⓪ 1   2   3

5. Designing buildings, bridges, or other structures ⓪ 1   2   3

*6. Developing methods of long-range weather fore-
    casting and prediction ⓪1   2   3

*7. Operating an x-ray machine or other laboratory
    apparatus ⓪1   2   3

*8. Examining the formation of mineral deposits and
    determining how they may be removed from the
    earth .... ⓪ 1   2   3

9. Programming computers to solve complex tech-
    nical problems .... ⓪ 1   2   3

10. Studying the causes of or diagnosing and treating
    diseases and physical impairments in humans or
    animals .... 0 ① 2   3

11. Navigating a ship or an airplane .... ⓪ 1 2 3

12. Developing mathematical equations or chemical formulas to solve scientific problems .... ⓪ 1 2 3

13. Studying the solar system .... 0 ① 2 3

14. Investigating water bodies, such as lakes, rivers, and oceans .... ⓪ 1 2 3

"0"

Sum of circled "1's"

Sum of circled "2's"

Sum of circled "3's"

Grand total of circled "1's," "2's," "3's"

| 0 |
| + |
| + |
| + |
| = |

My Artistic (A) Interests are in . . .

*1. Playing musical instruments in a band, orchestra, or other musical organization and/or writing music .... 0 1 ② 3

2. Designing floorplans and selecting furniture and color combinations for homes or offices .... 0 ① 2 3

3. Illustrating or designing covers for books or magazines .... 0 ① 2 3

4. Engaging in creative dance, ballet, or rhythmic gymnastics .... 0 1 2 ③

*5. Drawing cartoons, comics, or caricatures of people .... 0 ① 2 3

6. Writing short stories, novels, plays, or poetry .. 0 1 2 ③

7. Using wood, clay, paint, or other materials to create art objects .... 0 1 2 ③

*8. Doing creative photography .... 0 1 2 ③

9. Conducting an orchestra or directing a play .... ⓪ 1 2 3

10. Giving presentations or writing descriptions or criticisms of sculpture, plays, books, movies, or music .... 0 1 2 ③

11. Setting up art, merchandise, or museum displays .... ⓪ 1 2 3

*12. Writing dialogue or commercial announcements for radio or TV programs .... 0 ① 2 3

13. Studying and interpreting foreign languages ... 0 1 ② 3

14. Designing containers for commercial products .. ⓪ 1 2 3

"0"   ☐ 0

+

Sum of circled "1's"   ☐

+

Sum of circled "2's"   ☐

+

Sum of circled "3's"   ☐

=

Grand total of circled "1's," "2's," "3's"   ☐

My Social (S) Interests are in . . .

1. Supervising activities at parks or recreational facilities .... ⓪ 1 2 3

*2. Taking care of children and assisting in their education .... 0 ① 2 3

3. Helping people with their personal problems and important decisions in life .... 0 1 2 ③

4. Teaching or helping people to develop their talents and interests .... 0 1 2 ③

5. Teaching others how to care for themselves and improve their health .... 0 1 2 ③

*6. Advising parents about the rearing of their children .... ⓪ 1 2 3

7. Coordinating health and social services for the public .... 0 ① 2 3

8. Working with or helping in the treatment of sick, handicapped, or injured individuals .... 0 ① ② 3

*9. Supervising the selection, placement, and promotion of employees .... ⓪ 1 2 3

*10. Visiting homes to help people who are in trouble or need assistance .... ⓪ 1 2 3

11. Teaching arts and crafts to others .... ⓪ 1 2 3

12. Studying the customs and folkways of different societies and cultures .... ⓪ 1 2 3

13. Interviewing people for information about their beliefs and habits .... 0 1 2 ③

14. Helping others to develop their physical talents and athletic skills .... 0 1 ② 3

"0" $\boxed{0}$
+
Sum of circled "1's" $\boxed{}$
+
Sum of circled "2's" $\boxed{}$
+
Sum of circled "3's" $\boxed{}$
=
Grand total of circled "1's," "2's," "3's" $\boxed{}$

My Enterprising (E) Interests are in . . .

1. Managing my own firm 0 (1) 2 3

2. Buying and selling stocks and bonds .... (0) 1 2 3

*3. Buying merchandise for a large store or chain of stores .... (0) 1 2 3

4. Managing the public affairs division of a corporation .... (0) 1 2 3

5. Helping others to locate and secure equipment . (0) 1 2 3

6. Lobbying for the passage of a law .... (0) 1 2 3

7. Settling disputes between labor and management .... (0) 1 2 3

*8. Managing or directing a large enterprise or division of a corporation .... (0) 1 2 3

9. Directing a social service or recreational agency   0 1 (2) 3

*10. Directing the sales policies for a large firm or managing a group of salespeople .... (0) 1 2 3

11. Helping individuals plan their travels .... (0) 1 2 3

12. Making announcements on radio or television .. 0 (1) 2 3

*13. Investigating legal situations and interpreting the law .... (0) 1 2 3

14. Managing and representing performers, speakers, and artists .... (0) 1 2 3

"0"   [0]

                                                        +

Sum of circled "1's"   [   ]

                                                        +

Sum of circled "2's"   [   ]

                                                        +

Sum of circled "3's"   [   ]

                                                        =

Grand total of circled "1's," "2's," "3's"   [   ]

My Conventional (C) Interests are in . . .

1. Operating office machines .... (0) 1 2 3

2. Developing an accounting or filing system for a firm .... (0) 1 2 3

3. Posting bills for a large company .... (0) 1 2 3

4. Planning or coordinating a conference or convention 0 1 (2) 3

5. Assisting others in planning and managing their finances .... (0) 1 2 3

6. Classifying orders, figuring price quotations, and making out price sheets .... (0) 1 2 3

7. Keeping financial records .... (0) 1 2 3

8. Answering the telephone and giving information or routing phone calls .... (0) 1 2 3

9. Teaching business classes .... (0) 1 2 3

*10. Preparing payrolls, figuring commissions, and making salary deductions .... (0) 1 2 3

*11. Meeting clients, making appointments, and doing general office work 0 (1) 2 3

12. Taking dictation and typing correspondence ... (0) 1 2 3

*13. Making bookkeeping entries or keeping inventories .... (0) 1 2 3

14. Studying how people manage their time and energies to complete work tasks 0 (1) 2 3

"0"   [0]

                                                +

Sum of circled "1's"   [   ]

                                                +

Sum of circled "2's"   [   ]

                                                +

Sum of circled "3's"   [   ]

                                                =

Grand total of circled "1's," "2's," "3's"   [   ]

Check to make sure you have circled a number (0, 1, 2, 3) next to each item. Then add the scores in each Holland category and write the totals in the spaces provided. For example, in the Realistic category you would total all of the "1's" (if you had circled three of the "1's" the sum would be 3), all of the "2's" (if you had circled three of the "2's" the sum would be 6), and all of the "3's" (if you had circled three of the "3's" the sum would be 9). Next, add the three sums together to get your grand total for that category (from the above examples: 3 + 6 + 9 = 18).

After you have determined the grand totals for each of the six interest categories, transfer those totals to the spaces provided below. If, as in the example above, your grand total were 18 in the Realistic category, you would write 18 above the R space provided below).

Interest
grand   _11_   _5_   _23_   _16_   _4_   _4_
totals   R   I   A   S   E   C

FUNCTIONAL SKILLS

"Jim and Julia are the math whizzes in our class." "Tina and Bill are the class leaders." Statements such as these are often used to group individuals according to a common skill that they possess, many times because they excel at that skill. While we may not be outstanding at a particular task when compared to our peers, each of us possesses skills that will allow us to function effectively at particular work tasks.

Like the preceding assessment of your interests, this inventory requires that you look through several sets of Functional *Skills* and evaluate yourself on a scale that runs from "3" to "0."

Circle "3" next to an activity if you have a definite strong skill in that area 0 1 2 (3)

Circle "2" if you have a moderate degree of skill in that activity 0 1 (2) 3

Circle "1" to indicate that you have enough skill to get by with some help from others 0 (1) 2 3

Circle "0" if you believe you have no skill at all at that particular activity .... (0) 1 2 3

When evaluating your skills do not compare yourself with any particular reference group such as other students or the general population. Rate yourself according to your own judgment of your ability. Be sure that each item has a number circled beside it before moving to the next item.

My Realistic (R) Functional Skills are in . . .

*1. Painting, varnishing, or staining wood or metal surfaces 0 1 2 3

2. Working with wood using power tools, hand tools, or other woodworking equipment 0 1 2 3

3. Working outdoors for long periods of time 0 1 2 3

4. Putting together toys, furniture, or machinery that become unassembled 0 1 2 3

5. Repairing furniture or other objects 0 1 2 3

*6. Cleaning, adjusting, or repairing electric motors, sewing machines, or bicycles 0 1 2 3

7. Completing tasks that require physical endurance or agility 0 1 2 3

8. Making clothes or other wearing apparel from patterns 0 1 2 3

9. Driving a tractor or a truck 0 1 2 3

10. Reading blueprints or schemata 0 1 2 3

*11. Doing odd jobs with a saw, hammer and nails, screwdriver, or plane 0 1 2 3

*12. Making drawings with a compass, triangle, ruler, or other instruments 0 1 2 3

13. Installing or repairing household electrical circuits 0 1 2 3

14. Constructing, planting, or cultivating rock gardens or making flower beds 0 1 2 3

"0"   ☐ 0
                                              +

Sum of circled "1's"   ☐
                                              +

Sum of circled "2's"   ☐
                                              +

Sum of circled "3's"   ☐
                                              =

Grand total of circled "1's," "2's," "3's"   ☐

My Investigative (I) Functional Skills are in . . .

1. Mixing chemicals according to formulas 0 1 2 3

2. Experimenting with and creating recipes 0 1 2 3

3. Naming basic foods and telling why they are nutritious 0 1 2 3

4. Reading data tables, graphs, and charts 0 1 2 3

5. Setting up a scientific demonstration for a class or science fair 0 1 2 3

6. Understanding articles in newspapers and magazines about recent scientific breakthroughs 0 1 2 3

7. Describing the different classification systems for plants or animals 0 1 2 3

8. Reading topographical or navigational maps 0 1 2 3

9. Naming the different cloud formations 0 1 2 3

10. Using a microscope 0 1 2 3

11. Using a slide rule or hand calculator 0 1 2 3

12. Interviewing others about their attitudes, feelings, and beliefs 0 1 2 3

13. Solving puzzles or figuring out how things work 0 1 2 3

14. Identifying the major constellations of the stars . 0 1 2 3

"0" | 0 |

                                                        +

Sum of circled "1's" | |

                                                        +

Sum of circled "2's" | |

                                                        +

Sum of circled "3's" | |

                                                        =

Grand total of circled "1's," "2's," "3's" | |

My Artistic (A) Functional Skills are in . . .

1. Sketching, drawing, or painting; carving or sculpting objects 0 1 2 3

2. Creating new ideas and gadgets or expressing myself in original ways 0 1 2 3

3. Doing interpretive readings of stories, poetry, or plays 0 1 2 3

4. Impersonating the speech and mannerisms of others 0 1 2 3

5. Using the color wheel to mix colors or create color compliments 0 1 2 3

6. Writing essays, stories, or poetry 0 1 2 3

7. Designing and making clothing 0 1 2 3

8. Singing or acting 0 1 2 3

*9. Arranging color harmonies and furnishings in a home 0 1 2 3

10. Learning a foreign language 0 1 2 3

11. Playing a musical instrument 0 1 2 3

12. Following the story line and message in movies, plays, and books 0 1 2 3

13. Performing ballet, tap dance, or gymnastics 0 1 2 3

14. Telling stories or jokes 0 1 2 3

"0" $\boxed{0}$

+

Sum of circled "1's" $\boxed{}$

+

Sum of circled "2's" $\boxed{}$

+

Sum of circled "3's" $\boxed{}$

=

Grand total of circled "1's," "2's," "3's" $\boxed{}$

My Social (S) Functional Skills are in . . .

1. Performing in athletic competition 0 1 2 3
2. Planning social events 0 1 2 3
3. Entertaining others 0 1 2 3
4. Getting along with others who are different from myself...................................... 0 1 2 3
5. Teaching or tutoring 0 1 2 3
6. Explaining new ideas to others 0 1 2 3
7. Supervising children's activities 0 1 2 3
8. Meeting new people 0 1 2 3
9. Accepting and giving criticism 0 1 2 3
10. Helping others feel comfortable in new situations 0 1 2 3
11. Encouraging and supporting others 0 1 2 3
12. Working with others in a team effort 0 1 2 3
13. Determining the needs of others and helping them find solutions to their problems 0 1 2 3
14. Understanding other people's personalities 0 1 2 3

"0"
$\boxed{0}$

+

Sum of circled "1's"
$\boxed{}$

+

Sum of circled "2's"
$\boxed{}$

+

Sum of circled "3's"
$\boxed{}$

=

Grand total of circled "1's," "2's," "3's"
$\boxed{}$

My Enterprising (E) Functional Skills are in . . .

1. Organizing campaigns for candidates in school clubs or other social groups 0 1 2 3

2. Leading others 0 1 2 3

3. Entering new situations with ease and comfort .. 0 1 2 3

4. Interpreting changes in the economy 0 1 2 3

5. Persuading others to follow a new idea 0 1 2 3

6. Performing effectively in debates 0 1 2 3

7. Managing or supervising others in a work group 0 1 2 3

8. Selling products 0 1 2 3

9. Speaking in behalf of a group 0 1 2 3

10. Helping others find resolutions for their disputes 0 1 2 3

11. Understanding how the legal system operates and how laws are passed 0 1 2 3

12. Finding and capitalizing on bargains and sales .. 0 1 2 3

13. Soliciting contributions to charities or political organizations 0 1 2 3

14. Giving speechs before a large group 0 1 2 3

"0" | 0 |
                                                   +
Sum of circled "1's" | |
                                                   +
Sum of circled "2's" | |
                                                   +
Sum of circled "3's" | |
                                                   =
Grand total of circled "1's," "2's," "3's" | |

My Conventional (C) Functional Skills are in . . .

1. Operating office machines 0 1 2 3

2. Planning a personal budget 0 1 2 3

3. Organizing or filing materials such as records, class
    notes, stamps, or photographs 0 1 2 3

4. Keeping financial records 0 1 2 3

5. Typing, keypunching, or operating a calculator or
    office machine 0 1 2 3

6. Keeping an accurate checkbook 0 1 2 3

7. Organizing ideas or numbers so they are clear and
    understandable 0 1 2 3

8. Proofreading papers or records and finding the
    mistakes 0 1 2 3

9. Spelling and using punctuation and grammar
    correctly 0 1 2 3

10. Keeping accurate records 0 1 2 3

11. Examining or keeping budgets for businesses ... 0 1 2 3

12. Working in an office setting and doing a good
     job 0 1 2 3

13. Organizing my time to accomplish tasks 0 1 2 3

14. Acting as a secretary or treasurer in a club or
     organization 0 1 2 3

"0"   ☐ 0

+

Sum of circled "1's"   ☐

+

Sum of circled "2's"   ☐

+

Sum of circled "3's"   ☐

=

Grand total of circled "1's," "2's," "3's"   ☐

As you did with the Interest Inventory, go back and add the 1's, 2's, and 3's you have circled for each category of interest. Record the results in the spaces provided at the end of each category. After you have determined the grand totals for each of the six skill categories, transfer these totals to the spaces provided below. Record the grand totals in the appropriate spaces.

Functional
skills
grand   _____ _____ _____ _____ _____ _____
totals   R   I   A   S   E   C

SUMMARY PROFILES

The final step in this self-assessment process will be to pull together a composite picture of your interests and functional skills. Doing so will allow you to look at your interests and skills separately and to compare interest and skill areas with each other.

To complete this process, write the grand total of your interest scores and the grand total of your functional skill scores in the spaces provided below. Then, add the grand totals together to develop an overall composite score of your interests and functional skills.

	R	I	A	S	E	C
Interest grand totals	—	—	—	—	—	—
Functional skill grand totals	+	+	+	+	+	+
	—	—	—	—	—	—
	=	=	=	=	=	=
Overall composite score	□	□	□	□	□	□
	R	I	A	S	E	C

Lastly, write the letters (R, I, A, S, E, C) that correspond to your three highest (including tied highest) composite scores in the spaces provided below.

Summary Profile: — — —

Using the Summary Profile to Explore College Majors

Turn to the majors finder in the pages that follow and look for majors that correspond to the three letters in your summary profile. Be sure to rotate codes—for example, RIA, AIR, RAI, IRA, IAR, ARI. List the majors that have some appeal to you on the lines provided below.

1. _____

2. _____

3. _____

4. _____

5. _____

6. _____

7. _____

8. _____

9. _____

10. _____

Interpreting Your Summary Profiles

In addition to using the summary profile to identify majors for exploration, there are several other things to consider in looking at your summary profiles. First, are your interests and abilities consistent with each other? That is, do your highest interest scores correspond to your strongest abilities? If they do, it suggests that you like and do well at certain things and will probably have a relatively easy time entering majors and occupations that utilize these skills and interests. If your interests are substantially greater than your abilities, it suggests that you may need to find new ways of developing or refining your skills if you choose to pursue your interests; for example, by taking some refresher or basic background classes in your areas of interest. Conversely, if your abilities are greater than your interests in certain areas, it may suggest that there are some things you do well at but may not really invest yourself in on a contiuing basis. You may be good at a variety of office practices or conventional activities, for example, because you developed these to help you with your studies or for summer jobs, but you may not want to make a living with these skills on a permanent basis. Let's suppose further, that your interests were in the investigative and artistic areas. Given this situation, you may wish to consider the possibility of combining your interests and skills by utilizing your current skills in settings that are consistent with your interests; for example, in a medical or scientific setting or an advertising office, while you work to advance your education. In this way you can use your current skills to support yourself as you develop skills in areas that appeal to you.

It is also possible that all three letters have an equal score. This type of profile can occur in two ways: (1) all of your scores are high, suggesting that you have diverse talents and interests, and (2) all of your score are low, indicating that you have not fully developed your talents and interests. In the case of equally high scores you have several options to consider. You can look for majors and occupations that provide you with a great deal of diversity, or seek opportunities to work across a variety of settings. You can also identify the specific skills and interests you want to capitalize on and look for related majors or occupations. Or you can look at the idea of pursuing several fields during the course of your career, which will allow you to capitalize on your talents and interests in different ways across time. Lastly, you may explore the possibility of pursuing some activities at work that appeal to you and others outside of work, through leisure and recreational pursuits.

A low profile with equal scores may indicate that you haven't had opportunities to try out the kinds of diverse activities that would allow you to clearly identify your interests and talents. In this case, you may want to gain more experience through volunteer work, classes, and part-time or summer jobs in areas that appeal to you. This type of profile may also suggest that you may be resistant to any type of a career commitment right now, and need to explore what is happening in your life that makes you want to postpone such a commitment. It's not uncommon, for example, for students to feel that if they did what they wanted, they'd disappoint someone who is important to them, or if they tried and failed they wouldn't know how to cope with it. These and other thoughts, feelings, and conflicts may be best worked through with the assistance of a professional counselor. Your instructor may have some ideas on where such assistance can be found.

C

The Majors Finder

Realistic Areas
Investigative Areas
Artistic Areas
Social Areas
Enterprising Areas
Conventional Areas

Realistic Areas

3–Letter Code and Area of Study	Degrees
RIA	
Architectural Drafting	Tech
Dental Technology	Tech
RIS	
Agricultural Wood Science Technology	Tech
Forestry	Tech, BS
Forestry Management	BS
Forest Resources	BS
Forest Science	BS
Industrial Arts Education	BS
Industrial Design	BA
Optician	Tech
Resource Development	BS
Skilled Trades	Tech
Soil Reclamation and Conservation	Tech
Trade and Industrial Education	BS
RIE	
Agriculture	Tech, BS, MS, PhD
Agricultural Business Technology	Tech
Agricultural Engineering	BS, MS, PhD
Agricultural Industries	BS
Agricultural Mechanics and Systems	BS
Agricultural Products Technology	Tech
Agricultural Science	BS
Air Traffic Control	Tech
Auto Body Repair	Tech
Automotive, Diesel, and Gas Turbine Repair	Tech
Automotive Engineering	BS
Broadcast Technology	Tech
Civil Engineering	BS, MS, PhD
Civil Technology	Tech
Crop Product Technology	Tech
Dairy Products Technology	Tech
Drafting	Tech
Engineering Mechanics	BS, MS, PhD
Floriculture Technology	Tech
Food Processing Technology	Tech
Horticulture	Tech
Industrial Engineering	Tech, BS, MS, PhD
Livestock Production Technology	Tech

Realistic Areas

3–Letter Code and Area of Study	Degrees
Machine Operator	Tech
Mechanical Engineering	Tech, BS, MS, PhD
Nuclear Engineering	BS, MS, PhD
Ornamental Horticulture	Tech
Plant Sciences Technology	Tech
Plumbing	Tech
Poultry Production	Tech
Systems Engineering	BS
Welding Engineering	Tech, BS
RIC	
Fish Culture Technology	Tech
Instrumentation Technology	Tech
Marine Life Technology	Tech
Nuclear Technology	Tech
Nursery Operations Technology	Tech
Ocean Fishing Technology	Tech
Optical Technology	Tech
Plant Science Technology	Tech
Textile Technology	Tech
Turf Grass Management	Tech
Wildlife and Conservation Technology	Tech
REI	
Airconditioning, Heating and Refrigeration Technology	Tech
Typesetter	Tech
RES	
Fish and Game Warden	Tech
Park and Recreation Land Management	Tech

Investigative Areas

IAS	
Anatomy	MS, PhD
Economics	BS, MA, PhD
Economic Geography	BS
Economics and Statistics	BS, MA
Internal Medicine	MD
Labor Economics	BS

Investigative Areas

IAR

Anthropology	BA, MA, PhD
Astronomy	BS, MS, PhD
Biological Conservation	BS, MS, PhD
Biological Sciences	BS, MS, PhD
Biophysics	BS, MS, PhD
Chemical Physics	BS, MS, PhD
Chemistry	BS, MS, PhD
Engineering Physics	BS, MS, PhD
Medical Microbiology	MS, PhD, MD
Pathology	BS, MS, PhD
Physics	BS, MS, PhD
Veterinary Pathobiology	BS, MS, PhD

ISE

Institutional Leadership	BS

ISC

Medical Laboratory Assisting	Tech
Production Planning	BS

ISR

Biology	BS, MS, PhD
Developmental Biology	BS, MS, PhD
Environmental Biology	BS, MS, PhD
Environmental and Natural Resource Technology	Tech
Environmental Health Technology	Tech
Genetics	BS, MS, PhD
Mathematics Education	BS
Mathematical Sciences	BS, MS, PhD
Medical Microbiology	BS, MS, PhD
Microbiology	BS, MS, PhD
Natural Science Education	BS
Optometry	OD
Ophthalmology	MD
Osteopathy	MD
Physiological Optics	BS, OD
Recreation and Parks Technology	Tech

ISA

Anesthesiology	MS, MD
Circulation Technology	BS

Investigative Areas

Gynecology	MD
Inhalation Therapy Technology	Tech
Medical Assistant Technology	Tech
Medical Technology	BS
Medicine	MD
Nurse Anesthesiology	RN, Certified
Obstetrics	MD
Pediatrics	MD
Physician's Assistant	Tech
Psychiatry	MD
Psychology	BS, MS, PhD
Respiratory Technology	Tech, BS
Preventive Medicine	MD

IEC

Actuary Science	BS
Biostatistics	BS, MS, PhD
Statistics	BS, MS, PhD

IES

Anatomy	MS, PhD
Bacteriology	BS, MS, PhD
Microbiology	BS, MS, PhD
Pharmacy	BS, MS, PhD
Physiological Chemistry	BS, MS, PhD
Physiology	BS, MS, PhD
Veterinary Physiology and Pharmacology	MS, PhD

ICR

Agricultural Inspection and Quality Control	Tech
Agricultural Science Technology	Tech
Computer and Information Science Technology	Tech
Quality Control Technology	Tech

IRA

Geology	BS, MS, PhD
Mathematics, Statistics	BS, MS, PhD
Surgery	MD
Meteorology	BS
Weather Observation	BS

Investigtive Areas

IRS

Aboricultural Technology	Tech
Agronomy	BS, MS, PhD
Agriculture Business Management Technology	Tech
Agriculture Business Technology	Tech
Agriculture Entomology	BS, MS, PhD
Agriculture Food Science	BS, MS, PhD
Agriculture Products Technology	Tech
Agriculture Mechanics and Engineering Technology	Tech
Animal Science	BS, MS, PhD
Animal Sciences Technology	Tech
Biochemistry	BS, MS, PhD
Crime Lab Technology	Tech
Dairy Food Processing	Tech, BS, MS, PhD
Dairy Technology	BS
Emergency Medical Technology	Tech
Entomology	BS, MS, PhD
Environmental Biology	BS, MS, PhD
Floriculture	BS
Floriculture Technology	Tech
Fruit and Vegetables Processing Technology	Tech
Geodetic Science	BS, MS, PhD
Geography	BS, MS, PhD
Horse Management Technology	Tech
Horticulture	BS, MS, PhD
Landscape Horticulture	BS
Landscape Technology	Tech
Livestock Product Technology	Tech
Natural Resources	BS, MS
Nursery	BS
Oceanography Technology	MS, PhD
Plant Health and Protection Technology	Tech
Plant Nutrition Technology	Tech
Plant Pathology	BS, MS, PhD
Pomology	BS
Population and Environmental Biology	BS, MS, PhD
Radiology	MD
Radiologic Technology	Tech, BS
Respiratory Technology	Tech, BS

Investigative Areas

Soil and Water Engineering Technology	Tech
Vegetable Production	BS
Veterinary Anatomy	DVM, MS, PhD
Veterinarian Medicine	DVM
Veterinary Clinical Services	DVM
Veterinary Parasitology	DVM, MS, PhD
Veterinary Pathobiology	DVM, MS, PhD
Veterinary Preventive Medicine	DVM
Veterinary Technology	Tech
Waste Disposal Technology	Tech
X-Ray Technology	Tech
Zoology	BS, MS, PhD

IRE

Aeronautical and Astronautical Engineering and Technology	Tech, BS, MS, PhD
Aerospace Engineering and Technology	Tech, BS, MS, PhD
Agriculture Business Management Technology	Tech
Agricultural Chemicals Technology	Tech
Agricultural Mechanics and Engineering Technology	Tech
Animal Sciences Technology	Tech
Biomedical Engineering	BS
Ceramic Engineering	BS, MS, PhD
Chemical Engineering and Technology	Tech, BS, MS, PhD
Dentistry	DDS
Electrical Engineering and Technology	Tech, BS, MS, PhD
Electronics Technology	Tech
Metallurgical Engineering and Technology	Tech, BS, MS, PhD
Radio and Television Engineering	BS
Soil and Water Engineering Technology	Tech
Sound Engineering	BS
Veterinary Technology	Tech

IRC

Agricultural Equipment Technology	Tech
Airplane Navigation	BS
Allied Agricultural Research and Laboratory Science	Tech
Aviation	Tech, BS
Computer and Information Science	Tech, BS, MS, PhD
Histologic Technology	Tech
Laboratory Technology	Tech

Artistic Areas

AIR

Architecture	BS, MA
Art	BA, BFA, MA
Art Education	BS, MA, PhD
Audio–Visual Technology	Tech
City and Regional Planning	Tech, MA, PhD
Drawing–Painting	BA
Fine Arts	BA, BFA
Graphics	Tech, BA, BFA
History of Art	BA
Landscape Architecture	BS
Photography and Cinema	Tech, BA, BFA
Product Design	BA
Sculpture	BA, BFA
Space and Enclosure Design	BA
Visual Communication and Design	BA

AIS

Acting	BS
Agriculture Communications	BS
Broadcast Communications	BA
Ceramic Art	BA, BFA
Communication	BA
Fashion Design	Tech
Furniture Design	BS
Industrial Design	BA, MA
Interior Design	Tech
Islamic Studies	BA
East Asian Language and Literature	BA, MA, PhD
English	BA, MA, PhD
Jewish Studies	BA
Journalism Graphics	BA
Medical Communications	BS
Medical Illustration	BS
Theater	BA, BFA, MA, PhD
Visual Communication and Design	BA

AIE

Ceramic Art	BA
Decorator	Tech

Artistic Areas

ASE

Agriculture Communications	BS
Arabic	BA
Broadcast Journalism	BA
Chinese	BA
Commercial Art	Tech, BA
Dance Education	BS
Drama	BA
English Education	BS
Foreign Languages	BA
Journalism	BA
Linguistics	BA, MA, PhD
News–Editorial Journalism	BS
Public Relations	BS
Dance	BA, BFA
Romance Languages Literature	BA, MA, PhD
Russian	BA
Slavic Languages and Literature	BA, MA, PhD
Spanish	BA

ASI

Music	Tech, B. Mus
Art Education	BS
Ceramic Art	BA
Church Music	B. Mus
Drawing–Painting–Graphics	BA, BFA
English Education	BS
Music	Tech, BA, MA, PhD
Music Education	BS
Philosophy	BA, MA, PhD
Sculpture	BA, BFA

AES

Advertising	BA
Marketing	BS
Public Relations	BA

Social Areas

SRI

Agriculture Education	BS, MS, PhD
Dairy Technology	BS
Poultry Science	BS, MS, PhD
Home Economics Vocational Education	BS

SRE

Agriculture Education	BS, MA, PhD
Community Health	BS
Mental Health Technician	Tech
Occupational Therapy	Tech, BS
Operating Room Technician	Tech
Physical Education	BS, MA, PhD
Health Education	BS, MA, PhD

SIR

Environment Education	BS
Orothodontist	Tech
Physical Therapy	Tech, BS
Podiatry	BS
Pratestist	Tech
Urban Planning	Tech

SIA

Agriculture Social Sciene	BS
Black Studies	BA, MA
Industrial Sociology	BA
Islamic Studies	BA
Jewish Studies	BA
Nursing	Tech, RN, BS
Political Science	BA, MA, PhD
Rehabilitation Counselor	MA, PhD
Rural Sociology	BS
Social Science	BS
Social Science Education	BS, MA, PhD
Social Welfare Assistant	Tech
Social Work	BS, MA, PhD
Sociology	BS, MA, PhD
Latin American Studies	MA, PhD
Russian Studies	MA, PhD
Transnational Intellectual Corporation	MA, PhD
Women's Studies	BA

Social Areas

SIE

Dietetics	BS
Public Administration	MA, PhD
Manpower and Labor Relations	BS, MBA, PhD
Labor and Human Resources	BS, MBA
General Home Economics	BS
Home Economics	Tech, BS, MS, PhD
Home Economics Education	BS
Home Training Consultant	BS
House Equipment and Furnishings	BS
International Studies	BA
Restaurant Management	BS
Russian	BA
Spanish	BA
Speech Education	BS
Textiles and Clothing	BS

SIC

Educational Administration	MA, PhD
Education	BS
Law	JD
Corrections Specialist	Tech
Criminology	BS, MA, PhD
Police Science	Tech
Social Science Education	BS, MA, PhD

SAI

Blind and Partially Seeing Education	BS
Communications	BA
Dental Assisting	Tech
Dental Hygiene	Cert. DH, BS, BA
Dental Hygiene Education	BS
Deaf and Hard of Hearing Education	BS
Elementary Education	BS
Exceptional Children Education	BS, MA
Library Science	BS
Secondary Curricula	BS
Speech Communications	BA
Speech and Hearing Science	BA
Mentally Retarded	BS, MA

SAE

Arabic	BA

Social Areas

Chinese	BA
Clothing	BS
Consumer Services	BS
Dietetics and Institutional Management	BS
Education	BS, MA, PhD
Family and Child Development	BS
Food and Nutrition	BS
Foreign Language Education	BS
Fruit and Vegetable Processing	BS

SEI

Ancient History and Classics	BA, MA, PhD
Classics	BA
Educational Administration	MA, PhD
History	BA, MA, PhD
Medical Dietetics	BS
Medieval and Renaissance	BA
Social Science Education	BS
Consumer Services	BS

SEA

Community Recreation Administration	BS
Foreign Trade Specialty	Tech
Home Furnishings Speciality	Tech
International Studies	BA
Public Recreation	Tech, BS
Guidance and Counseling	MA, PhD
Psychology	BS, MA, PhD

SEC

Food Science and Nutrition	BS
Food Technology	Tech, BS
Funeral Service Director	Tech
Hotel and Restaurant Management	Tech
Residence Hall Director	BA, MA
Social Work	BS, MA, PhD
Manpower and Labor Relations	BS, MBA, PhD

SCE

Business Education	BS
Distributive Education	BS
Dietetics and Institutional Management	BS
Public Recreation	BS

Social Areas

Hotel and Restaurant Management	Tech, BS
Medical Record Administration	BS
Manpower and Labor Relations	BS, MBA, PhD
Recreation Director	BS

Enterprising Areas

ECI

Banking	BS
Marketing	Tech, BS, MBA, PhD

ECS

Insurance and Risk	BS, MBA, PhD
Real Estate	Tech, BS, MBA, PhD
Retailing	Tech

ERI

Agricultural Economics	BS, MS, PhD
Dairy Science	BS, MS, PhD
Industrial Engineering	BS, MA, PhD
International Agriculture	BS

EAS

Law	JD
Radio and Television Broadcasting	Tech

EAR

Radio and Television Broadcasting	Tech

ESC

Fisheries and Wildlife Management	BS
Hospital and Health Services Administration	MS, MBA
Industrial Relations	BA
Institutional Leadership	MA, PhD
Insurance and Risk	BS, MBA, PhD
Manpower and Labor Relations	BS, MBA, PhD
Parks and Recreation Administration	BS
Production and Operations Management	BS, MBA, PhD
Public Administration	MA, PhD
Restaurant Management	BS
Transportation and Logistics	BS, MBA, PhD

Enterprising Areas

ESI

Insurance Investigation	Tech
Institutional Management	Tech
International Business Administration	BS
Insurance and Risk	BS, MBA, PhD
Manpower and Industrial Relations	BS, MBA, PhD
Management Science	Tech, BS, MA, PhD
Public Administration	Tech, MA, PhD
Systems Engineering	BS, MA, PhD

ESA

Airline Stewardess	Tech
Fashion Merchandising	Tech
Public Recreation	BS

Conventional Areas

CRI

Keypunch Operator	Tech

CIS

Accounting	Tech, BS, MA, PhD

CSA

Court Reporting	Tech
General Secretary	Tech
Legal Secretary	Tech
Library Technical Assistant	Tech
Medical–Dental Secretary	Tech
Medical Records Technician	Tech

CSE

Business Education	BS, MA, PhD
Personnel Clerk	Tech

CER

Data Processing	Tech

CEI

Finance	BS, MBA, PhD

Conventional Areas

CES

Accounting	BS, MBA, PhD
Banking and Finance	Tech, BS
Business Administration	Tech, BS, MBA, PhD
Business Administration, Cooperative Programs	BS
Force and Policy—Internal and External Security	MA, PhD
Hospital and Health Services Administration	MS, MBA

Appendix

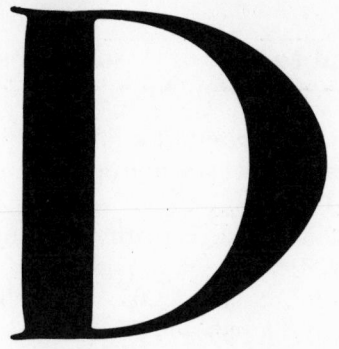

A Partial Listing of Professional and Trade Associations

A Partial Listing of Professional and Trade Associations

Occupation	Organization and Address
Accountants	American Institute of Certified Public Accountants, 1211 Avenue of the Americas, New York, N.Y. 10036
Actors and Artists	Associated Actors and Artists of America, 165 W. 46th St., New York, N.Y. 10036
Actuaries	Society of Actuaries, 208 S. LaSalle St., Chicago, Ill. 60604
Advertising Workers	American Advertising Federation, 1225 Connecticut Ave., N.W., Washington, D.C. 20036
Aircraft Industries	Aerospace Industries Association of America, 1725 DeSales St., N.W., Washington, D.C. 20036
Airline Workers	Air Transport Association of America, 1000 Connecticut Ave., Washington, D.C. 20036
Architects	American Institute of Architects, 1735 New York Ave., N.W., Washington, D.C. 20036
Architects, Landscape	American Society of Landscape Architects, 1750 Old Meadow Rd., McLean, Va. 22101
Astronomers	American Astronomical Society, 211 Fitz Randolph Rd., Princeton, N.J. 08540
Bakers	American Bakers Association, Suite 650, 1700 Pennsylvania Ave., N.W., Washington, D.C. 20006
Bankers	American Bankers Association, 90 Park Ave., New York, N.Y. 10016
Barbers and Beauty Operators	Associated Master Barbers and Beauticians of America, 219 Greenwich Rd., P.O. Box 17782, Charlotte, N.C. 28211
Bricklayers	Structural Clay Products Institute, 1750 Old Meadow Rd., McLean, Va. 22101
Broadcasters	National Association of Broadcasters, 1771 N St., N.W., Washington, D.C. 20036
Building Trades	AFL and CIO Building and Construction Trades Dept., 815 16th St., N.W., Washington, D.C. 20006
Chemists	American Chemical Society, 1155 16th St., N.W., Washington, D.C. 20036

Occupation	Organization and Address
Chiropractors	International Chiropractors Association, 741 Brady St., Davenport, Iowa 52805
Coal Mining	National Coal Association, 1130 17th St., N.W. Washington, D.C. 20036
Compositors	Printing Industries of America, Inc., 5223 River Rd., N.W., Washington, D.C. 20016
Data Processors	Data Processing Management Association, 505 Busse Hwy., Park Ridge, Ill. 60068
Decorators	American Institute of Interior Decorators, 730 Fifth Ave., New York, N.Y. 10019
Dental Assistants	American Dental Assistants Association, 211 E. Chicago Ave., Chicago, Ill. 60611
Dental Hygienists	American Dental Assistants Association, 211 E. Chicago Ave., Chicago, Ill. 60611
Dental Technicians	National Association of Certified Dental Laboratories, 1330 Massachusetts Ave., N.W., Washington, D.C. 20005
Dentists	American Dental Association, 211 E. Chicago Ave., Chicago, Ill. 60611
Dieticians	American Dietetic Association, 620 N. Michigan Ave., Chicago, Ill. 60611
Ecology Workers	Ecological Society of America, Dept. of Botany, Southern Illinois University, Carbondale, Ill. 62901
Economists	American Economic Association, 1313 21st Ave., S., Nashville, Tenn. 37212
Electrical Workers	International Brotherhood of Electrical Workers, 1200 15th St., N.W., Washington, D.C. 20005
Engineers, Aeronautical	American Institute of Aeronautics and Astronautics, 1290 Avenue of the Americas, New York, N.Y. 10019
Engineers, Agricultural	American Society of Agricultural Engineers, 2950 Niles Rd., St. Joseph, Mich. 49085
Engineers, Ceramic	American Ceramic Society, 4055 N. High St., Columbus, Ohio 43214
Engineers, Chemical	American Institute of Chemical Engineers, 345 E. 47th St., New York, N.Y. 10017

A Partial Listing of Professional and Trade Associations

Occupation	Organization and Address
Engineers, Civil	American Society of Civil Engineers, 345 E. 47th St., New York, N.Y. 10017
Engineers, Electrical	Institute of Electrical and Electronics Engineers, 345 E. 47th St., New York, N.Y. 10017
Engineers, Industrial	American Institute of Industrial Engineers, 345 E. 47th St., New York, N.Y. 10017
Engineers, Marine	American Society of Naval Engineers, Inc., 1012 14th St., N.W., Suite 807, Washington, D.C. 20005
Engineers, Mechanical	American Society of Mechanical Engineers, 345 E. 47th St., New York, N.Y. 10017
Engineers, Mining, Metallurgical, and Petroleum	American Institute of Mining, Metallurgical, and Petroleum Engineers, 345 E. 47th St., New York, N.Y. 10017
Engineers, Radio	Institute of Electrical and Electronics Engineers, 345 E. 47th St., New York, N.Y. 10017
Farmers	U.S. Dept. of Agriculture, Washington, D.C. 20250
Florists	Society of American Florists and Ornamental Horticulturists, 901 N. Washington St., Alexandria, Va. 22314
Foresters	Society of American Foresters, 1010 16th St., N.W., Washington, D.C. 20036
Forge Shop Workers	Forging Industry Association, 55 Public Square, Cleveland, Ohio 44113
Funeral Directors and Embalmers	National Funeral Directors Association of the U.S., 135 W. Wells St., Milwaukee, Wis. 53203
Geographers	Association of American Geographers, 1146 16th St., N.W., Washington, D.C. 20036
Geologists	American Geological Institute, 1444 North St., N.W., Washington, D.C. 20005
Hairdressers and Cosmetologists	National Hairdressers and Cosmetologists Association, 175 Fifth Ave., New York, N.Y. 10010
Home Economists	American Home Economics Association, 1600 20th St., N.W., Washington, D.C. 20009

Occupation	Organization and Address
Hospital Workers	American Hospital Association, 840 N. Lake Shore Dr., Chicago, Ill. 60611
Hotel Workers	American Hotel and Motel Association, 221 W. 57th St., New York, N.Y. 10019
Insurance Agents	National Association of Insurance Agents, 96 Fulton St., New York, N.Y. 10038
Jewelers and Jewelry Repairers	Retail Jewelers of America, 1025 Vermont Ave., N.W., Washington, D.C. 20005
Lawyers	American Bar Association, 1155 E. 60th St., Chicago, Ill. 60637
Librarians	American Library Association, 50 E. Huron St., Chicago, Ill. 60611
Machinists, all-around	International Association of Machinists, 1300 Connecticut Ave., Washington, D.C. 20036
Mathematicians	Mathematical Association of America, SUNY at Buffalo, Buffalo, N.Y. 14214
Mechanics, Refrigeration and Air Conditioning	United Association of Journeymen, Apprentices of Plumbing and Pipe Fitting Industries, 901 Massachusetts Ave., Washington, D.C. 20001
Medical Laboratory Technicians	Registry of Medical Technologists, American Society of Chemical Pathologists, P.O. Box 2544, Muncie, Ind. 47302
Medical Record Librarians	American Medical Record Association, 875 N. Michigan Ave., Chicago, Ill. 60611
Medical X-Ray Technicians	American Society, Radiologic Technicians, 537 S. Main St., Fond Du Lac, Wis. 54935
Meteorologists	American Meteorological Society, 45 Beacon St., Boston, Mass. 02108
Microbiologists	American Society for Bacteriology, 1913 Eye St., N.W., Washington, D.C. 20006
Musicians	American Federation of Musicians, 641 Lexington Ave., New York, N.Y. 10022
Nurses, Practical	National Association for Practical Nurse Education and Service, Inc., 1465 Broadway, New York, N.Y. 10036
Nurses, Registered	National League for Nursing, 10 Columbus Circle, New York, N.Y. 10018
Occupational Therapists	American Occupational Therapy Association, 251 Park Ave., South, New York, N.Y. 10010

A Partial Listing of Professional and Trade Associations

Occupation	Organization and Address
Opticians	Optical Society of America, 2100 Pennsylvania Ave., N.W., Washington, D.C. 20037
Optometrists	American Optometric Association, 7000 Chippewa St., St. Louis, Mo. 63119
Osteopathic Physicians	American Osteopathic Association, 212 E. Ohio St., Chicago, Ill. 60611
Petroleum Workers	American Petroleum Institute, 1271 Avenue of the Americas, New York, N.Y. 10020
Pharmacists	American Pharmaceutical Association, 2215 Constitution Ave., Washington, D.C. 20037
Photographers	Professional Photographers of America, 1090 Executive Way, Oak Leaf Commons, Des Plaines, Ill. 60018
Physical Therapists	American Physical Therapy Association, 1790 Broadway, New York, N.Y. 10019
Physicians	American Medical Association, 535 N. Dearborn St., Chicago, Ill. 60610
Physicists	American Institute of Physics, 335 E. 45th St., New York, N.Y. 10017
Plastics Workers	Society of the Plastics Industry, 250 Park Ave., New York, N.Y. 10017
Plumbers and Pipe Fitters	United Association of Journeymen, Apprentices of Plumbing and Pipe Fitting Industries, 901 Massachusetts Ave., N.W., Washington, D.C. 20001
Podiatrists	American Podiatry Association, 20 Chevy Chase Circle, N.W., Washington, D.C. 20015
Psychologists	American Psychological Association, 1200 17th St., N.W., Washington, D.C. 20036
Public Relations	Public Relations Society of America, 845 Third Ave., New York, N.Y. 10022
Railroad Workers	Association of American Railroads, American Railroads Bldg., Washington, D.C. 20036
Real Estate Salesmen	National Association of Real Estate Boards, 155 E. Superior St., Chicago, Ill. 60611

Occupation	Organization and Address
Recreation Workers	National Recreation and Park Association, 1700 Pennsylvania Ave., N.W., Washington, D.C. 20006
Restaurant Workers	National Restaurant Association, 1530 N. Lake Shore Dr., Chicago, Ill. 60610
Retail Grocers	National Association of Retail Grocers of the United States, 360 N. Michigan Ave., Chicago, Ill. 60601
Secretaries	National Secretaries Association, 616 E. 63rd St., Kansas City, Mo. 64110
Social Workers	National Commission for Social Work Careers, 2 Park Ave., New York, N.Y. 10016
Sociologists	American Sociological Association, 1772 N. St., N.W., Washington, D.C. 20036
Speech Therapists	American Speech and Hearing Association, 9030 Old Georgetown Road, Washington, D.C. 20014
Teachers	National Center for Information on Careers in Education, 1607 New Hampshire Ave., N.W., Washington, D.C. 20009
Television and Radio Workers	American Federation of Television and Radio Artists, 724 Fifth Ave., New York, N.Y. 10022
Textile Workers	American Textiles Association, 1501 Johnston St., Charlotte, N.C. 28202
Truckers	American Trucking Association, 1616 P St., N.W., Washington, D.C. 20036
Veterinarians	American Veterinary Medical Association, 600 S. Michigan Ave., Chicago, Ill. 60605
Welders	American Welding Society, 2501 N.W. 7th St., Miami, Fla. 33125

For additional listings of professional and trade associations see:

Carrol Press Staff. *Career Guide to Professional Associations.* Cranston, R.I.: Carroll Press, 1976.

C. Colgate, Jr., and G.J. Slagle (Eds.), *National Trade and Professional Associations of the United States and Canada and Labor Unions.* Washington, D.C.: Columbia Books, Inc., 1976.

Index